*Milestones to
Shakespeare*

Milestones to Shakespeare

A study of the dramatic forms and pageantry
that were the prelude to Shakespeare.

By

David Klein, Ph.D. 1880 -

Professor Emeritus of English,
City College of New York

Twayne Publishers, Inc.   ::   New York

37359

To My Wife

KATE

CONTENTS

Milestones to Shakespeare

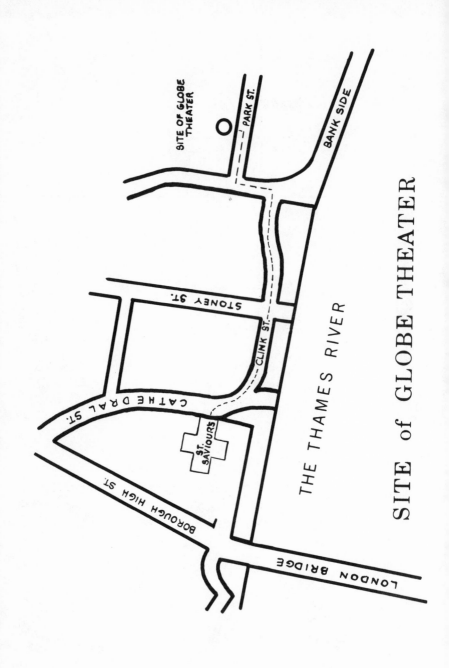

SITE of GLOBE THEATER

I.   THE BIBLE PLAY 1

In the Middle Ages dramatic entertainment in Europe was of two kinds: that which was in some way connected with the religious and educational efforts of the church, and that which was of secular origin. The latter included all sorts of wayside entertainment, supplied by strolling professionals, such as tumbling, juggling, conjuring, puppetry, and slapstick farce, forms of recreation that have come down in an unbroken tradition to our own time, when they found a respectable home in the vaudeville house, and, with the passing of that, on television. It also included folk plays indulged in by the country people in their holiday merrymakings. It is to such plays that Perdita, in Shakespeare's *Winter's Tale,* refers when she says:

> Methinks I play as I have seen them do
> In Whitsun pastorals.

In England, the favorite hero in these popular plays was Robin Hood.

Of the other kind of dramatic entertainment, namely, that connected with the church, there were three types: the Miracle Play, the Bible Play, and the Morality. A Miracle Play was a dramatization of an episode in the life of a saint. A Bible play (frequently known as a Mystery) was a dramatization of an episode in the Bible. A Morality was an allegorical play in which the characters were personifications of ideas, feelings, or qualities, such as Conscience, Folly, Experience, Pity, Riches, Diligence, and so forth. One play of this type, named *Everyman,* was rendered widely popular at the beginning of this century by a revival of it staged by Mr. Ben Greet. It roused so much interest that it prompted the writing of two modern imitations entitled, respectively, *Everywoman* and *Experience,* both of which were successful on Broadway.

The Miracle Play did not achieve great popularity in England, hence not a single complete specimen in English has come down to us. In fact, its very name has been commonly applied to the Bible Play. The latter had its beginnings in the attempt to present important events in the history of Jesus in an interesting, attractive and intelligible form. One of the most important events in that history was the resurrection. During the Easter service the choir chanted the following dialogue based on the Gospel of Mark: "Whom seek ye in the sepulchre, O Christians?" "Jesus the Nazarene who was crucified, O heavenly ones." "He is not here; he is arisen as he foretold; go ye, proclaim that he is arisen." Since this was chanted in Latin most of the congregation had not the faintest notion of what it meant. Accordingly, a dramatic device was resorted to about the ninth century. A portion of the altar was fitted up to resemble a sepulchre. Into this, on Good Friday, a crucifix, wrapped in linen, was deposited in the presence of the worshipers. On the morning of Easter Sunday, before the congregation arrived, the crucifix was removed. What occurred during the following service was a little play, which may be most concisely and effectively described in the very words, in translation, of the original ecclesiastical direction, dating from the tenth century: "While the third lesson is being read, let four friars clothe themselves, and let one of them, dressed in a white alb, go secretly to the sepulchre, and there sit quiet holding a palm. When the third Responsory is over let the remaining three follow, walking as if they were looking for something. When the first sees them approaching, let him begin to chant in a subdued, sweet voice: 'Whom seek ye in the sepulchre, O Christians?' Let them respond: 'Jesus the Nazarene, who was crucified, O heavenly ones.' Then he: 'He is not here; he is arisen as he foretold.' " To prove his statement he is directed to broadly display the empty linen.

A scene like this the people could understand; they liked it, and wanted more of the same kind. Hence not only did the presentation become more elaborate, but additional episodes concerned with the last days of Jesus were similarly dramatized. In this way, what may be called an Easter cycle grew up. In like manner, there developed a group of plays concerned with the nativity of Jesus, to be performed at Christmas time.

Such plays were simple enough; but they were real plays. The name commonly given to them is Liturgical Plays, because of their connection with the divine service. In introducing them into the service the clergy, as Professor Oscar Cargill has shown, secured the services of professional entertainers. Professional entertainers there always were—wandering minstrels, and strolling vagabonds, that roamed over the country, and lived by their wits—a disreputable lot. Specimens of the tribe are the two rapscallions that fastened themselves upon poor Huckleberry Finn, and called themselves respectively the Duke and the Dauphin.

Inglorious lot as they were, they share the credit for the creation of the earliest form of drama in Europe after the decline of the ancient world. They also share the credit for the creation of the first popular drama in modern Europe. The liturgical plays cannot be called popular plays. To begin with, they were written and chanted in Latin. What the crowd understood was only what could be perceived through the eye. The possibilities of a richer development were practically nil. The interest in them was primarily religious, not theatrical. In some parts of Europe some of them have survived as religious ceremonies down to our own day. The point need not be urged that before a drama can be considered a living institution, with vital potentialities, it must be composed in the vernacular—the language of the people. With the assistance of the professional entertainers such a drama was established. The transition was accomplished through the medium of the Crusades.

Every army has its camp-followers, who eke out an existence by catering to the needs and pleasures of the soldiers. The multitudes that thus followed the crusading hosts could be counted by the hundred thousand; and among them were the vagabond entertainers. Among the things that they saw in the East were religious plays given in the language of the people; for in the East, Latin never became the official language of the church. We may be sure that when the hosts returned to Europe they brought with them the desire for such plays, and that they would instill that desire in those that had stayed at home.

We presently find, all over Europe, a sudden expansion of the Bible play. No longer was it brief, and limited to a few episodes in the New Testament; it covered in the fullest detail all the episodes in the life of Jesus, and even some of the events recorded in the Old Testament, and in legend. No longer was it chanted in Latin by the clergy; it was spoken in the vernacular by a cast drawn from the people—and among the performers were professional actors. No longer was it given as part of the divine service, each episode on its appropriate day; it was planned as one grand continuous performance of a sequence of plays, usually out of doors.

The conception that determined the plan was a magnificent one. The great Christian epic of the redemption of man was to be presented in dramatic form. Hence most of the plays were based upon the New Testament. However, the design not only permitted, but required the introduction of Old Testament material. The redemption presupposed a fall; consequently the story of Adam and Eve had to be included. There were other episodes, too, in the Old Testament, that bore a definite theologic relation to the New Testament—those of the flood, and the sacrifice of Isaac, for example. Indeed, the composer might even find it necessary to go back of the Old Testament, for the creation of man was motivated by the fall of the angels. Accordingly, the cycle was very apt to begin with the revolt of Lucifer. At the other end, the divine scheme would be consummated by the enactment of the Day of Judgment. This was a long program, which sometimes required several days to complete.

The manner of staging had great significance in the light of later developments. The stage was a long platform—not too high, for the actors made use of the ground also. On the platform was erected a series of pavilions and doorways, representing the successive places where the scene of action was laid. In one of the extant pictures of a medieval stage we see heaven on the roof of a pavilion at one end, and hell at the other end. Hell was in the shape of a horrible monster's head, with opening and closing jaws, through which issued fire and smoke. It was always placed on or near the ground, so that the devils might run out and scurry through the audience, to the latter's great terror and delight. If some bad boy dared trespass on the area reserved for the actors, hell-mouth would open, and out would rush a devil, who would carry the kicking rascal into hell, and let him out through the rear—or possibly set him to work pumping the bellows that manufactured the smoke.

Sometimes the stage consisted of a series of platforms ranged around the public square. In England the favorite method was to erect a movable float for each playlet, and have the floats move in rotation to different stations throughout the city. Each play would thus be performed as many times as there were stations. In York there were twelve such stations. Obviously, the houses whose windows looked out upon the stage enjoyed a special advantage. In York, therefore, and probably elsewhere, the selection of locations was determined by auction. This peripatetic method of production solved the problem of congestion.

The idea was probably hit upon because in those towns where it was put into practice the production was not undertaken by the whole community acting as a unit. Instead, each play was assigned to a particular guild, which would thus build its own stage. Sometimes there was a distinct appropriateness in the assignment. For example, *The Building of the Ark* went to the shipwrights, *The Flood* to the mariners and the fishmongers, *The Crucifixion* to the pinners and the butchers, the *Harrowing of Hell* to the cooks.

The staging was quite elaborate. There were tunnels, trap-doors, dragons, whirling angels of fire, thunder, and similar devices. Compartments could be made to open and close. The item of expense entailed by painting was relatively high. Special pains were taken with paradise. One scene builder proudly pointed to the work he had just completed, and said: "Look! there is the most beautiful paradise you ever saw," and added, "or that you ever will see."

The acting was good, the actors being carefully selected, and well trained, possibly by professional actors, who would also assume difficult roles. Heavy fines were imposed for absence from rehearsal; and one Harry Cowper, a weaver of Beverly, was fined six shillings and eight pence for not knowing his part.

The first important thing to note about the plays thus produced is that they were a communal affair. They were written for the people, because the people demanded them, and were acted by the people. The days set aside for their performance were among the longest of the year, and were charged with a holiday spirit, the folk from all the country 'round pouring into town. The next important thing to note is that since the plays owed their existence to a popular demand, they were bound to become the expression of the life of the people. How that could happen with plays based on material so far removed from the joys and sorrows of our workaday world, may be hard to see. That it did happen will be demonstrated in the next chapter, where we shall be introduced to one or two dramatic geniuses of the fourteenth century—worthy forerunners of William Shakespeare.

II.   THE BIBLE PLAY 2

In the last chapter it was indicated that since the Bible plays owed their existence to a popular demand, they were bound to become the expression of the life of the people, notwithstanding the apparently remote character of the basic material of which they were made. The fact is that to the unsophisticated masses of the Middle Ages, the stories of the Bible were not distantly removed from the joys and sorrows of their daily life. The biblical personages were not remote and shadowy phantoms. They were conceived as human beings, of flesh and blood, who lived much as men and women of their own day lived, and whose favorite oath was "By St. John"—that is, if they belonged to the righteous; if they belonged to the wicked they swore by Mahomet (an obvious reflection of the Crusades). The charming anachronism only emphasizes the realism which was an outstanding characteristic of these plays. A brief examination of two or three of them will illustrate.

In the play concerning the Deluge, for example, Noah is, of course, a righteous, God-fearing man, as the Bible tells us. But he is also a husband. Had Mrs. Noah nothing to say in the matter? The Bible doesn't tell us. But the married men of the Middle Ages didn't have to be told. They had definite ideas of what to expect in such a situation, and the playwright gave them what they expected. Thus the play became a comedy of domestic conflict.

It opens with the Lord expressing his regret that he ever created man, and announcing his decision to destroy him—that is, all except Noah and his family. He thereupon pays Noah a visit, and gives him the necessary instructions for building the ark. Noah does not seem awestruck by the divine audience he has been granted. He is merely humbly appreciative of the Lord's condescension:

> I thank thee, Lord so dear,
> That would vouchsafe
> Thus low to appear
> To a simple knave.

It may be noted in passing that in this matter of goodnatured familiarity between the Lord and Noah, the twentieth-century successful Bible plays, *Noah* and *Green Pastures,* merely fall in line with tradition.

No sooner is Noah alone than he realizes that he must break the news to his wife. He anticipates trouble from that quarter—and he is not disappointed. When the ark is built (we see it done in a few minutes) Mrs. Noah scornfully refuses to enter. She expresses the most wholesome contempt for her husband as a marine architect:

> I was never barred ere
> In such a cage as this.
> In faith, I cannot find
> Which is before, which is behind.
> Shall we here be penned!

Noah begs her to desist, lest the spectators think that she is master—and in an undertone he ruefully admits: "And so thou art, by St. John."

The storm is rising. The thunder rolls ominously. Drops are beginning to come down. Noah gets terribly excited, and calls to his wife:

> Behold to the heaven!
> The cataracts all,
> They are open full even,
> Great and small;
> And the planets seven
> Have left their stall;
> This thunder and lightning
> Down make fall
> Full stout,
> Both halls and bowers,
> Castles and towers:
> Full sharp are these showers
> That run about!
> Therefore, wife, have done—
> Come into ship, fast!

But she doesn't share his excitement at all. All the rejoinder he can get is:

> Yea, Noah, go clout thy shoes;
> The better will they last.

In despair, he turns to the spectators:

> Ye men that have wives!
> Whilst they are young
> If you value your lives,
> Chastise their tongue.
> Methinks my heart rives
> To see such strifes
> Wed men among.

Presently Mrs. Noah is willing to compromise. She agrees to enter the ark if her husband agree to admit all her cronies:

> They shall not drown, by St. John,
> If I may save their life.

Of course that stipulation cannot be considered.

The three sons appeal to her, each in turn. The three daughters-in-law appeal to her, each in turn. In vain! Words proving of no avail, Noah decides to use force. He gets as good as he gives, and a rough and tumble fight ensues. (Remember that Mrs. Noah's part was also taken by a man). Finally, all three sons seize their mother and deposit her in the ark. Noah bids her welcome, and in return he gets a wallop in the face. All he can say is: "Marry, this is hot."

At this point the stage direction reads:

> Then shall Noah shut the window of the ark, and for a
> little space be silent, and afterwards, looking about,
> shall say: "Now forty days are fully gone."

And the spectators promptly realized that the "little space" of silence was equivalent to forty days.

What we have covered of the play sufficiently emphasizes certain features which are commonly considered distinguishing characteristics of the Elizabethan drama. There is a frank disregard of the limitations of time. A "little space" is accepted as forty days. There is a startling commingling of the comic with the serious. There is intimacy between actor and spectator. Noah does not hesitate to speak directly to the audience. And there are the innocent anachronisms which resulted from the contemporary spirit in which the play was conceived, and which gave it homely reality.

If *The Deluge* is a domestic comedy, our second play, *The Sacrifice of Isaac,* is a domestic tragedy. It is the story of a broken-hearted father and a frightened child, whose last thought before the expected blow, and whose first thought after the rescue, is of his mother. The pathos is genuine.

The boy gaily carries the wood for the sacrificial fire. Not till he reaches the altar does he realize that there is something wrong. He is disturbed by the expression on his father's face:

> Why make you so much heavy cheer?
> Are you anything adread?
> Father, where is the beast that we shall kill?
> Father, I am full sore afraid
> To see you bear this drawn sword!
> I hope you will not slay your own child!

The agonized father breaks the truth to him, and the boy pleads:

> Alas! What have I done?
> If I have trespassed in any degree,
> With a yard you may beat me.
> Put up your sword,
> For I am but a child.
> > *Abraham:* My child, I may not choose.
> > *Isaac:* Now I would to God my mother were here!
> She would kneel for me on both her knees
> To save my life.
> And since my mother is not here,
> I pray you, father, change your cheer,
> And kill me not.

When he learns that it is God's will, he is resigned, and thinks only of the grief of his parents. He does his best to comfort his father:

> > *Isaac:* Ye have other children
> The which ye should love.
> I pray you, father, make ye no woe,
> For be I once dead and from you gone,

I shall be soon out of your mind.
But, good father, tell ye my mother nothing;
Say that I am in another country dwelling.
If she wot it she would weep full sore,
For iwis, father, she loved me full well,
God's blessing may she have;
I come no more under her wing.
Farewell forever and aye!

He does not hear the angel's voice forbidding Abraham to strike. When he finally realizes that he is safe, he exclaims:

Lord God! I thank Thee with all my heart;
For I am glad that I shall live
And kiss once more my dear mother.

The best of all the Bible plays is the comedy episode attached to the play depicting the Adoration of the Shepherds in the so-called Towneley Cycle. Indeed, this fourteenth century play is the best play Europe had produced in over fifteen hundred years; that is, since the days of Terence, and England was to wait nearly two hundred years more before producing its equal. It would be futile to attempt in the space at my disposal to give anything like adequate illustration of the richness of its dialogue and the vigor of its humor.

In this play we again find an admirable example of the realism that governed the medieval playwright's conception of his work. The subject is the annunciation to the shepherds and their subsequent adoration. Yet it is not till the very end that this subject is brought in at all. Most of the play is a vividly realistic presentation of an episode in shepherd life. Three shepherds chance to meet in the fields and, of course, get to talking about their troubles. They unpack their hearts with complaints—complaints about the weather, which has been cold and nasty, about their employers, who withhold their wages, about the gentry generally, who take unfair advantage of them in every possible way. They find solace in food and song.

A new character now comes upon the scene, in the form of a notorious thief named Mak. They are tired and sleepy, but are now afraid to fall asleep. The only thing they can do is to have Mak lie between them. Mak has no difficulty, however, in getting up when they fall asleep and stealing "a good fat sheep." He takes the sheep home and knocks on the door. He gains a grudging admittance from his wife, who grumbles about the way she is overworked. However, she changes her tune when she sees what her husband has brought: "Ah, come in, sweeting!" Knowing that the shepherds will suspect him and come to his house in search of the sheep, Mak becomes panicky. His wife contemptuously tells him that if *he* hasn't the brains to think of a good trick, *she* has. "Yet a woman's wit helps at the last." She will hide the sheep in the cradle, and pretend that she has just given birth to a baby.

The trick works—almost. The shepherds search high and low, and finally conclude that this time they have accused Mak unjustly. They are already at the door, when they suddenly recall that they have left no present for the baby. Mak's heart drops to his boots. He begs them not to disturb the baby, but they insist on leaving sixpence in the cradle. Of course the sheep is discovered. The joke is too good for the shepherds not to enjoy it, and they have fun trying to discover a resemblance between Mak and his newborn heir. Their enjoyment, however, does not prevent them from giving Mak a good tossing in a blanket. At this point, with a sublime irrelevance, the angel is heard announcing the birth of the Redeemer, and the shepherds follow the Star to Bethlehem.

This is the barest outline of the plot, yet it suffices to indicate what a good play it is. Again we note the characteristics which we found illustrated in *The Deluge*. the realism, the juxtaposition of the sublime and the ridiculous, the naive disregard of what the classicists call the Unities of Time, Place, and Action; all of which characteristics were inherited by the great Elizabethan drama, in which we find sub-plots, frequent change of scene, and action covering long periods of time, sometimes many years.

The type of drama which we have been discussing was not destined to develop into a more modern form. Its career was effectually checked by the termination of the Middle Ages. The opening years of the modern age are known as the Renaissance because they were characterized by a violently awakened desire for new knowledge, illustrated, among other ways, by the discovery of America, and an avid interest in the products of

Greek and Roman culture. This interest amounted almost to worship. So unreasoning was it, that people began to despise the products of the Middle Ages. For example, the beautiful church architecture of the Middle Ages they scornfully named "Gothic," which to them was a synonym for "barbarous," and by that name has it been known to this day. Is it any wonder, then, that the much less perfect drama which the Middle Ages had produced should be neglected and allowed to perish? However, for centuries that drama had been molding the taste of the English public, and the greatness of the Elizabethan drama is in no small measure due to the fact that Shakespeare and his fellows accepted that taste and wrote accordingly, ignoring the laws that governed Greek and Roman drama.

III.   THE EARLIEST EXTANT MODERN PLAY

One fact made it inevitable that the medieval drama would be scornfully rejected by the Renaissance: it did not exist entirely for its own sake; it was the handmaiden of religion and morality. To teach these was its ostensible purpose. The element of entertainment was only incidental and, indeed, was frowned on by the clergy. The people of the Renaissance frankly wanted amusement. They rejected the medieval notion that pleasure was sinful. They believed in the joy of living, and sought ways and means of securing it. With such a spirit prevailing, it was inevitable that new types of drama should arise. Everywhere the production of plays of a secular character was stimulated, under the auspices, respectively, of professional actors in public places, of wide-awake schoolmasters in the schools, and of scholarly patrons in palaces and private homes.

The fullest records of such activity among the nobility naturally come from Italy. The local potentates in the different Italian cities vied with one another in dramatic entertainment, but in interest displayed and success achieved the Dukes of Ferrara easily led the rest. Ferrara was fortunate in boasting among its native sons the famous Lodovico Ariosto, author of the great romantic epic, *Orlando Furioso*. Besides being an epic poet, Ariosto was a playwright whose influence was a dominant one both at home and abroad. It is an interesting and significant fact that the English poet, Edmund Spenser, whose *Fairy Queen* bears so direct a relation to Ariosto's *Orlando Furioso* also wrote nine comedies (now lost) in imitation of Ariosto's comedies.

Precisely when and where the new drama began, and what its subsequent interrelations were, it is not easy to trace. It is generally assumed (probably a safe assumption) that it began in Italy and from there was carried abroad. Yet the data at our disposal are not sufficient to enable us to dogmatize on the subject. For instance, the play which has been called the first modern drama is Ariosto's *Cassaria,* acted in Ferrara in 1508. Yet within this generation an English play has come to light which was acted more than a decade earlier, namely, *Fulgens and Lucrece,* by Henry Medwall, chaplain in the household of Cardinal Morton. And there is evidence in it that such plays were not by any means new in England.

In a prologue a character called A, informed by B that a play was about to be acted, exclaims with delight:

> By my troth, thereof am I glad and fain;
> Of all the world I love such sport,
> It doth me so much pleasure and comfort;
> And that causeth me ever to resort
> Where such thing is to do.

And B assures him:

> I love to behold such mirths alway;
> For I have seen before this day
> Of such manner things in many a good place.

By "a good place" he means the home of a distinguished person.

Obviously then, Medwall did not give the world *Fulgens and Lucrece* as an experiment in something new. It simply happens to be the oldest extant. Plays were not the kind of literature that would be sedulously preserved.

Similarly, it is just as certain that Ariosto's *Cassaria* was not the first modern play written in Italy. We know that Ariosto himself composed plays when he was a boy, for himself and his brothers to act in at home. When a boy writes plays (or anything else, for that matter) he follows existing models. If we only had Ariosto's models! Thus the question of priority remains an open one.

However, one thing seems clear, namely, that the Englishman's enjoyment of plays was more intense than that of the Italian. Note, for instance, with what excitement the characters A and B above bubble over at the thought of dramatic entertainment. The Italian, apparently, could not accept the play unless it was interlarded with other types of entertainment, such as dances, masques, dumb shows, and the like. In one account after another of performances of Italian plays during this period, the delighted spectator dwells enthusiastically upon these *intermezzi,* as they were called, and makes only slight reference, if any, to the play proper. And these *intermezzi* were very apt to be so extensive as to take up most of the time. The

Italian, likewise, would be lavish in expenditure on the setting, even engaging great painters, like Raphael, to paint the scenery. The Englishman did not need these allurements. To him the play was the thing. The result was that Renaissance England developed a great drama, while Renaissance Italy did not.

Now we are ready to consider the oldest extant modern European play, just mentioned: Medwall's *Fulgens and Lucrece,* written under the patronage of Cardinal Morton. My readers will perhaps recognize Cardinal Morton as the Bishop of Ely, the memory of whose strawberries in Holborn made Gloucester's mouth water at a critical moment in Shakespeare's *Richard the Third.* He was an enthusiastic patron of letters, and under his aegis there grew up a literary coterie which made momentous contributions to the English drama. But of that later.

Fulgens and Lucrece is a romantic comedy that, with startling aptness, foreshadows the technique employed by Shakespeare. There is a main plot, more or less serious in tone, and a comic underplot. Fulgens, a Roman Senator, has a beautiful and virtuous daughter, who is courted by two desirable suitors—one a wealthy patrician, but pleasure-loving, the other a youth of virtue and industry, but of humble birth. The Senator is inclined to the patrician, but leaves the choice entirely to his daughter. While the two men woo the lady, their servants woo the maid. The plot is thus parallel to that of *The Merchant of Venice.* While Bassanio woos Portia, Gratiano woos Nerissa. The resemblance, however, stops with the general outline; it does not proceed to the details. In fact, the details are few.

The play was written for a performance at a banquet, probably a banquet given by Cardinal Morton. It opens with a prologue—the kind popularly employed by the Elizabethan playwrights, especially Ben Jonson. The guests have just finished the noonday meal (which has probably been protracted far into the afternoon) and are expectantly watching for the beginning of the play. A character named A—just plain capital A—enters, and expresses surprise at the reigning silence:

> Ah! for God's will,
> What mean ye, sirs, to stand so still?

> Have not ye eaten, and your fill,
> And paid nothing therefor?
> Iwis, sirs, thus dare I say,
> He that shall for the shot pay
> Vouchsafeth that ye largely assay
> Such meat as he hath in store.
> I trow your dishes be not bare;
> Nor yet ye do the wine spare;
> Therefore be merry as ye fare.
> Ye are welcome each one
> Unto this house, without feigning.

But this call to good cheer going unheeded, it dawns upon him that there must be some special reason for this persistent silence, and he is determined to find out what it is. Another character, named B, steps up from the audience, informs him that there is going to be a play, and proceeds to give him an outline of the story. A begins to criticize, but B shuts him up with the suggestion that he had better wait till he has seen the play before forming an opinion.

Senator Fulgens enters, and in a soliloquy of ninety lines tells us, amid much moralizing, that his cup of happiness would be completely filled if he could see his daughter suitably married before he died. Thereupon enters Publius Cornelius, the wealthy suitor, who begs him to intercede with his daughter in his behalf. The father agrees:

> Sir, I shall do you the comfort that I can
> As far as she will be advised by me.
> Howbeit, certainly, I am not the man
> That will take from her the liberty
> Of her own choice; that may not be.
> But when I speak with her I shall her advise
> To love you before other in all godly wise.

The impatient lover urges him to hasten on his mission.

Left alone, Publius Cornelius decides to engage a servant who will help him in his suit, so he asks the audience if there isn't someone among them who would be willing to take the job. B steps up and offers his services. Presently he advises A to take service with Gaius Flaminius, the rival suitor.

We next hear an interview between Senator Fulgens and his daughter Lucrece, the upshot of which is that the girl is to make a careful investigation as to which of the two suitors is the more honorable. The father makes his exit.

Hereupon enters Gaius Flaminius, who makes a manly and touching appeal for the young lady's hand. When she coyly asks him what he would with her, his earnest reply is:

> What need you then to ask the question
> What I would with you at this season?
> Meseemeth that ye should therein doubt no more,
> Since ye know well my errand before:
> Iwis, your strangeness grieveth me sore.
> But notwithstanding now will I cease,
> And at this time I will chide no more,
> Lest I give you cause of heaviness.
> I came hither only for your sake, doubtless,
> To glad you and please you in all that I can,
> And not for to chide with you, as I began.
> For think it in your mind, I am the man
> That would you please in all that I may,
> And to that purpose I will do what I can,
> Though you forbid it and say therein nay;
> In that point only I will you disobey.
> My heart shall ye have in all godly wise,
> Whether you me take or utterly despise.
> And to say that I will follow the guise
> Of wanton lovers nowaday,
> Which doth many flattering words devise,
> With gifts of rings and brooches gay
> Their lemans' hearts for to betray,
> Ye must have me therein excused,
> For it is the thing that I never used.
> Therefore I will be short and plain,
> And I pray you heartily, fair Lucrece,
> That ye will be so to me again.
> Ye know well that I have made labor and business,
> And also desired you by words express
> That ye would vouchsafe in your heart
> To be my wife till death us depart.
> Lo, this is the matter that I come for,
> To know therein your mind and pleasure,
> Whether ye set by me any store

> To the effect of my said desire:
> And nothing else I will require
> But that I may have a plain yea or nay,
> Whereto I may trust without delay.

She is moved and leaves him with the promise to accept him if her father consents.

Here the character named A steps up out of the audience and offers Flaminius his services. He is accepted after B vouches for him, and his first act of duty is to inform his master that he has a rival in Publius Cornelius. Flaminius' impatience increases as he recognizes the merits of his rival, so he sends A to Lucrece to get her decision as soon as possible.

At this point the author evidently felt that his audience needed relief—and it probably did after the long speeches to which it has been treated. Accordingly he sets his farcial sub-plot in motion. While A is off to get Lucrece's reply B makes love to Lucrece's maid Joan, whom he picturesquely calls "flower of the frying pan," and A returns just as he kisses her. A dispute arises, which is settled by Joan agreeing to accept the one that proves his superiority—superiority in anything—

> Be it cookery, or pastry,
> In feats of arms, or deeds of chivalry.

They try singing, then wrestling, but without any definite result. Finally they engage in a burlesque joust, in which A is overthrown. When B claims his reward, Joan announces that she is already engaged to another. When the rivals protest the unfair treatment, she gives them both a sound thrashing, and leaves them. When Flaminius enters and finds them in a sorry mess, they give him a Falstaffian account of a terrible battle they had fought for his sake. Then A reports Lucrece's decision; namely, that both rivals be given an opportunity to prove their respective claims by disputation, a very popular exercise in those days.

By this time the day has come to a close, so the play is interrupted to enable the guests to eat supper. That done, they are treated to a mumming, a species of ballet, ostensibly provided by Publius Cornelius, the wealthy suitor, for the delectation of Lucrece. We derive a vague notion of the nature

of the entertainment from some hints in the text. Cornelius asks
Lucrece: "Will ye see a base dance after the guise of Spain?" (a
base dance being a slow stately dance). Lucrece agrees, so he
orders the performers to come in, accompanied by the
minstrels. After the performance Lucrece's comment is:

> Forsooth, this was a goodly recreation.
> But I pray you, of what manner nation
> Be these godly creatures?
> Were they of England or of Wales?
>   *B.* Nay, they be wild Irish Portingales
> That did all these pleasures.

"All these pleasures" suggests variety. It would appear that they
belonged to the same category as the Italian *intermezzi,* and
performed the same function. The performers were a professional troupe open for engagements. In the first reference to
them in the play, the character A informs B that his master
Cornelius

> hath devised
> Certain strangers freshly disguised
> At his own expense
> For to be here this night also.
>   *A.* Strangers, quotha! what to do?
>   *B.* Marry, for to glad withal
> This gentlewoman at her hither coming.
>   *A.* Ah, then, I see well we shall have a mumming.
>   *B.* Yea, surely that we shall.

The mummers are called "strangers," because they were not
attached to Cardinal Morton's household; they were only
engaged for this special occasion. On the other hand, the actors
who performed in the play proper constituted a company that
formed a regular component of the domestic establishment. The
man who plays the part of A is the leader; he speaks of the
others as "my company."

In the scheduled debate that follows, Publius Cornelius, in a
speech nearly one hundred and fifty lines in length, claims
blood and wealth to his credit, while Gaius Flaminius, in a
speech almost as long, advances his own deeds. Lucrece
proclaims Flaminius the victor, at the same time assuring the
audience that she by no means scorned nobility of birth. She

affirms and reiterates that she fully knew the deference due a man of pedigree. To hold the matter of birth lightly would not do in Tudor England. She insists, moreover, that her verdict be strictly confined to the present case; it must, under no circumstances, be put down as a precedent.

So this is the earliest extant modern play in Europe. It is nothing to wax enthusiastic about, especially when compared with Bible plays that we have considered, like the play of Mak the sheep stealer, for example, written more than a century earlier. But we must not forget that those Bible plays were the product of a great literary age, an age that produced Chaucer, Gower, and Langland, while *Fulgens and Lucrece* is the product of the barren fifteenth century, a period that was too much occupied with wars to have time for the finer things. At the same time it must be conceded that its own merits as theatrical entertainment have been adequately demonstrated in college performances both in New York and in London. Its literary merit is small, the diction being frequently determined by the exigencies of the rhyme. But to the student of the theater it possesses other points of interest. It supplies evidence that the vogue of the secular drama was already a wide one, and was now old enough to have evolved a consciousness of the author's relation to his public. A various-minded audience must be pleased, explains the author:

> This was the substance of the play
> That was showed here today;
> Albeit that there was
> Divers toys mingled in the same
> To stir folk to mirth and game
> And to do them solace:
> The which trifles be impertinent
> To the matter principal,
> But nevertheless they be expedient
> For to satisfy and content
> Many a man withal.
> For some there be that looks and gapes
> Only for such trifles and japes,
> And some there be among
> That forceth little of such madness,
> But delighteth them in matter of sadness,

Be it never so long.
And every man must have his mind,
Else they will many faults find
And say the play was nought.
But, no force, I care not;
Let them say and spare not,
For God knoweth my thought.

This sounds like a fore-echo. Many Elizabethan dramatists expressed themselves similarly. The unknown author of the Morality play, *The Contention between Liberality and Prodigality*, stated the case this way:

The proverb is: How many men so many minds . . .
No play, no part, can all alike content.
The grave divine calls for divinity,
The civil servant for philosophy;
The courtier some rare sound history,
The baser sort for knacks of pleasantry.

Even the defiant thrust at the end of the quotation is matched again and again by Ben Jonson. Once he spat his scorn at his public in these insulting words:

But that I should plant my felicity in your general
saying good, or well, etc., were a weakness which the
better sort of you might worthily contemn, if not
hate, me for.

The student of the Elizabethan drama feels that he is already travelling over territory not altogether unfamiliar. The student of the general history of the theater will be impressed by the audience participation and the alphabetical designation of characters—features which he would associate with sophisticated ultra-modern theatrical experimentation.

IV.   THE ABORTED BIRTH OF THE MODERN DRAMA IN ENGLAND

We have extant a group of eleven plays which together constitute the English contribution to the earliest secular drama of modern Europe. They must be considered as a group, for they all emanated from a single coterie that flourished under the aegis of Cardinal Morton, Archbishop of Canterbury. Four members of the coterie (possibly only three) are responsible for the eleven plays referred to. These are: Henry Medwall, Sir Thomas More, his brother-in-law John Rastell, and Rastell's son-in-law John Heywood.

Thomas More and John Heywood are well known to readers. Less familiar figures are Henry Medwall and John Rastell. Henry Medwall we discussed in the last chapter, and analyzed his recently discovered play, *Fulgens and Lucrece,* which we called the earliest extant secular play in modern Europe. Medwall was also the author of the extant play entitled *Nature;* and we have no assurance that it was not written earlier than *Fulgens and Lucrece.* But a question might be raised whether *Nature* is an essentially secular play, inasmuch as it retains the form of the Morality Play, even though its substance is not treated from the standpoint of religion.

Medwall was the oldest member of the group, and both of his extant plays were written before 1500. The remaining nine were probably written some time during the first quarter of the sixteenth century, and used to be more or less indiscriminately ascribed to John Heywood, the youngest member of the group. Recent investigation, however, has proved this general ascription to be an error, three of the plays undoubtedly belonging to Heywood's father-in-law, John Rastell. For convenience sake it is worth while mentioning the titles. They are: *Of Gentleness and Nobility, The Four Elements,* and *Calisto and Meliboea.* The first two, like Medwall's *Nature,* are morality plays in form, but modern and scientific in spirit. The third is note-worthy because it is an adaptation of a Spanish play. In *Fulgens and Lucrece* Medwall had adapted an Italian source. Thus the first modern English playwrights set the example of going abroad for material, so avidly followed by their successors, Shakespeare and his fellows.

We haven't the space to go into details with these plays. Let it suffice to quote what Professor Tucker Brooke has to say about one of them: "The author of *Gentleness and Nobility* has a mastery of dramatic technique. The speakers are brought on and off the stage with perfect naturalness; the interplay of speech and action is that of the adept in arranging stage situation." A criticism like this would make the maturest playwright happy.

Now for the remaining six of the eleven plays. The titles and plots of three of them are well known to college students. All the textbooks on English literature lay stress upon them. These are: *The Four P's, The Pardoner and the Friar,* and *A Merry Play between John the Husband, Tyb his wife, and Sir John the Priest.* These are all living farces. The remaining three do not equal these, and their names are not generally familiar. They are: *The Play of Love, The Play of Weather,* and *Witty and Witless.* Yet it is only these three plays to which Heywood's claim cannot be contested. All three are antiquated in tone and manner, and only one of them, *The Play of Weather,* has any real dramatic interest. Tired of having everybody complain about the weather, Jupiter issues a proclamation that he will grant the complainants a hearing. Many come, including a boy, who wants a permanent snowfall.

After Jupiter has heard their conflicting requests, he points out first what he calls the "inconvenience" of having all kinds of weather, everywhere, at the same time. Then he points out the economic fact that everybody is dependent on everybody else; hence that each suitor present has been soliciting his own misfortune. Accordingly, he would grant each one his favorite weather during certain periods only. In other words, the weather would continue to be regulated just as it always had been. And everyone goes home happy.

Now for the remaining three, easily the best of the lot. Some time ago Dr. A. W. Reed made out an excellent case based on internal evidence, for the attribution of these lively farces to Sir Thomas More, yet he tentatively let *The Four P's* go to John Heywood. Later, apparently frightened by the startling character of his findings, he weakened, and took the position that all three were written by Heywood, but under More's influence. "I accept," he says, "Mr. Pollard's summary of my position." And this is Mr. Pollard's summary: "Mr. Reed would clearly be pleased if he could prove that the two farces were written by More himself, but he is content to regard them as Heywood's written under More's influence, and perhaps such a mixt authorship is the best solution."

If I may be allowed to express an opinion, I still think Dr. Reed's case for More's authorship a good one. I certainly find it difficult to believe that the author of the three recognized Heywood plays can be the author of the plays in question. There is a world of difference between them. What would check a scholar's ready acceptance of More's authorship is the fact that he would like to accept it; hence there would be danger that the wish would become father to the thought; and also the fact that there are no extant plays or titles of plays directly attributed to More. But we do know that More wrote plays. The great Erasmus, a friend of More, said so. His interest in the drama was a tradition—a tradition that was exploited by the authors of the Elizabethan play, *Sir Thomas More*. His dramatic inventiveness became strikingly evident in the report of his son-in-law, William Roper, to the effect that during the performance of plays in Cardinal Morton's home by professional players, young More would sometimes step in among the actors and create a part for himself extemporaneously, fitting it to the plot and dialog; and his improvisations afforded more entertainment than the original play. How inconclusive such speculations can be, however, is forcefully illustrated by the fact that Professor C. W. Wallace of the University of Nebraska, who may be credited with the most extensive researches of recent times in the area of the Elizabethan drama, ascribes the three plays concerned neither to Heywood nor to More, but to Henry the Eighth's choir master, William Cornish—of whom more later.

However, we are lucky to have the plays, though the authorship be in doubt. They are admirable imitations of French farces, reinforced plentifully with realistic borrowings from Chaucer. The plays are thus thoroughly English in spirit. I wish I had space to give extensive excerpts from all three, but I shall have to content myself with one—the best of them; namely, *A Merry Play between John the Husband, Tyb his Wife, and Sir John the Priest*. Here are the high spots. John comes home and finds that his wife, as usual, is out. He addresses the audience:

> *John.* Godspeed you, masters, everyone!
> Know ye not whither my wife's gone?
> I pray God the devil take her!
> But, by gog's blood, were she come home
> Unto this, my house, by our Lady of Crome,
> I would beat her ere that I drink.
> Beat her quotha? yea, that she shall stink!
> And at every stroke lay her on the ground,
> And drag her by the hair about the house round.
> I am just mad that I'm not beating her now.
> There was never a wife between heaven and hell
> Which was ever beaten half so well.

At this point his wife enters and overhears him.

> *Tyb.* Why, whom wilt thou beat, I say, thou knave?
> *John.* Who, I, Tyb? None, so God me save.
> *Tyb.* Yes, I heard thee say thou wouldst one beat.
> *John.* Marry, wife, it was stockfish in Thames Street,
> Which will be good meat against Lent.
> Why, Tyb, what hadst thou thought that I had meant?

Presently she informs him that she has a pie for dinner, and orders him to go to invite Sir John the Priest. With mouth watering in anticipation he starts off briskly, but she tantalizingly keeps calling him back until he has completed all the chores. Then she bursts upon him:

> What! art thou not gone yet out of this place?
> I had thought thou hadst come back in the space!
> But, by cock's soul, if I should do thee right,
> I should break thy knave's head tonight.
> *John.* Nay, then, if my wife be set achiding,
> It is time for me to go.
> There is a proverb which true now proveth:
> "He needs must go that the devil driveth."

He returns with Sir John and is thus greeted by his wife:

> The devil take thee for thy long tarrying!

> Here is not a whit of water, by my gown,
> To wash our hands that we might sit down.
> Go and hie thee as fast as a snail,
> And with fair water fill me this pail.

He hates to leave his wife alone with her guest. He goes, however, but returns with lively haste. The pail in his hand is empty, for there is a big hole in the bottom. She gives him a piece of hard wax and orders him to stand by the fire to soften it and mend the pail. He does as he is told, muttering all the while as he watches his wife and Sir John regaling themselves. Finally the pie is all eaten up, and John complains ruefully:

> Now our pie
> Is eaten up; there is not left a bit!
> And you two there do sit,
> Eating and drinking at your own desire,
> And I am John John, who must sit by the fire
> Chafing the wax, and dare none other do.
> But what! shall I anon go to bed
> And eat nothing, neither meat nor bread?
> I have not been wont to have such fare.

Now they proceed to mock him:

> *Tyb.* Why! were ye not served there as ye are
> Chafing the wax, standing by the fire?
> *John.* Why, what meat gave ye me, I you require?
> *Sir J.* Wast thou not served, I pray thee heartily,
> Both with the bread, the ale, and the pie?
> *John.* No sir, I had none of that fare.
> *Tyb.* Why, were ye not served there as ye are,
> Standing by the fire, chafing the wax?
> *John.* By cock's soul, they think I am either drunk or mad!
> *Tyb.* And had ye no meat, John John?
> *John.* No, Tyb, my wife; I had not a whit.
> *Tyb.* What, not a morsel?
> *John.* No, not a bit.
> For hunger, I trow, I shall fall in a swoon.
> *Tyb.* But is it true?
> *John.* Yes, for a surety.
> *Tyb.* Dost thou lie?

> *John,* No, so might I thrive!
> *Tyb.* Hast thou had nothing?
> *John.* No, not a bit.
> *Tyb.* Where wast thou?
> *John.* By the fire I did stand.
> *Tyb.* What didst?
> *John.* I chafed this wax in my hand,
> Whereas I know of wedded men the pain
> That they have, and yet dare not complain.

But now he does muster courage enough to dare. The worm turns:

> *John.* Since ye twain
> Will give me no meat,
> By cock's soul, I will take no longer pain!
> Ye shall do all yourself, with a very vengeance
> For me! And take thou there thy pail now,
> And if thou canst mend it, let me see how.
>> *(He throws the pail to floor.).*
> *Tyb.* Ah, knave! hast thou broke my pail?
> Thou shalt repent!
> Reach me my distaff, or my clipping-sheers!
> I shall make the blood run about his ears.
>> *(John takes up a shovelful of coals.)*
> *John.* Nay, stand still, drab, I say, and come not near:
> For, by cock's blood, if thou come here,
> Or if thou once stir toward this place,
> I shall throw this shovelful of coals in thy face!

The fight is on. The naive stage direction reads: *"Here they fight by the ears."* John gives a good account of himself. The enemy retreat, leaving John in triumphant possession of the field. And so the play comes to an end. For years to come, a fight, or a thrashing, was a favorite way of ending a play.

V. SCHOOL DRAMA

The year 1553 saw the appearance of two plays of high literary merit, each written by a schoolmaster for performance by his pupils, as part of their education. They stand out like twin peaks in a wide literary desert. One is entitled *Ralph Roister Doister,* the other, *Gammer Gurton's Needle.* The author of the former was Nicholas Udall; the latter is attributed on the title page of the first edition to Mr. S., whose identity is still in dispute. Udall's work has been incorrectly classified as an English adaptation of Plautus' Latin comedy, *The Braggart Warrior.* The indebtedness is limited to the portraits of the stupid, boastful soldier and his parasite. This is how Plautus introduces them to us:

Pyrgopolynices. Where is Artotrogus?

Artotrogus. He stands beside a man who's brave and blessed and beautiful as a prince; and as to your fame as a fighter—Mars himself wouldn't dare mention it, or compare his achievements with yours.

Pyrg. Was that the fellow I saved in the battle of Weevil Plains, where the commander in chief was Bumbomachides Clutomestoridysarchides, the grandson of Neptune?

Arto. Ah, I remember. You mean the one with the golden armor, whose legions you puffed away with a breath, just as the wind blows away leaves or a thatched roof.

Pyrg. That was a mere nothing.

Arto. A mere nothing, to be sure, compared with the other deeds I could mention . . . Gad! that elephant in India, for instance! How you smashed his forearm with your fist!

Pyrg. What! Forearm?

Arto. Foreleg, I meant to say.

Pyrg. I didn't hit very hard.

Arto. Of course not. If you had really put your strength into it, your arm would have transpierced the elephant all the way through, hide, flesh, bones, and all. *(Aside)* It's my belly that's responsible for all my sufferings. I have to 'ear him with my ears, so that my dental work can make dents in his food; and I have to agree to any lie he tells.

Pyrg. What was it I was saying?

Arto. Ah! I know already what you want to say. Heavens! You did it. I remember that you did it.

Pyrg. Did what?

Arto. Whatever it is you did.

Pyrg. Well, what do you recall?

Arto. Let me see. There were one hundred in Cilicia, one hundred and fifty in Sythobrigandia, thirty Sardians, sixty Macedonians—those are the men you slaughtered in one day.

Pyrg. And what's the sum total of men?

Arto. Seven thousand.

Pyrg. Yes, that's what it ought to be. Your calculation is quite correct . . . .

Arto. But why should I tell you what all mortals know, that you are the one and only Pyrgopolynices on earth, unsurpassed in valor, in beauty, and in brave deeds? All the women are in love with you, and not without reason, since you're so handsome. Take, for instance, those girls yesterday who caught me by the cloak.

Pyrg. What did they say?

Arto. They kept asking about you. "Is this fellow Achilles?" one of them says to me. "No," says I, "It is his brother." Then the other one says to me, "Dear me, but he's handsome, and such a gentleman, too. Just look how lovely his hair is. The women that sleep with him are certainly lucky."

Pyrg. Did they really say that?

Arto. Why, didn't both of them beg me to lead you past them today, as if you were on parade?

Pyrg. It's such a nuisance for a man to be so handsome.

Arto. Absolutely right, sir. They're a bother to me; they beg, urge, beseech to be allowed to see you; they keep sending for me, so that I can't devote myself to your business.

This dialogue Udall borrows—and improves upon. But this is where the indebtedness ends. From here on the Plautus play develops into a comedy of complicated intrigue, in which the braggart is subordinated, while Udall's proceeds along a succession of convincing situations, with the braggart as protagonist, to an hilarious climax—all in a natural English setting.

The Prologue announces the main intent of the play—entertainment; which distinguishes it from the medieval drama, whose main intent was instruction:

> What creature is in health, either young or old,
> But some mirth with modesty will be glad to use—
> As we in this interlude shall now unfold?

> Wherein all scurrility we utterly refuse,
> Avoiding such mirth wherein is abuse;
> Knowing nothing more commendable for a man's recreation
> Than mirth which is used in an honest fashion.
>
> For mirth prolongeth life, and causeth health;
> Mirth recreates our spirits, and voideth pensiveness,
> Mirth increases amity, not hindering our wealth . . . .

The first scene introduces us to the parasite, who is appropriately named Matthew Merrygreek, he tells us, because of his irrepressibly merry disposition:

> As long liveth the merry man, they say,
> As doth the sorry man, and longer by a day,
> Yet the grasshopper, for all his summer piping,
> Starveth in winter with hungry griping.

In other words, merriment isn't enough to fill the stomach.

> Yet wisdom would that I did myself bethink
> Where to be provided this day of meat and drink. . . .
> My living lieth here, and there; of God's grace
> Sometime with this good man, sometime in that place.

He proceeds to enumerate a list of neighbors on whom he sponges for his meals. Among them are such names as Lewis Loiterer, Watkin Waster, Nicol Neverthrive, Bryan Blinkinsop—names calculated to establish an earthy English atmosphere. There is no ancient Roman odor about it.

This day is Ralph Roister Doister's turn to be his host.

> For truly of all men he is my chief banker,
> Both for meat and money, and my chief sheet-anchor.

With the ingratitude of a parasite he proceeds to draw an uncomplimentary portrait of his patron:

> But now of Roister Doister somewhat to express,
> That ye may esteem him after his worthiness:
> In these twenty towns, and seek them throughout,
> Is not the like stock whereon to graff a lout.

All the day long is he facing and craking
Of his great acts in fighting and fraymaking;
But when Roister Doister is put to the proof,
To keep the Queen's peace is more for his behoof.
If any woman smile, or cast on him an eye,
Up is he to the hard ears in love by-and-by!
And in all the hot haste must she be his wife,
Else farewell his good days, and farewell his life!

His life is thus one endless repetition of falling in love; and, sure enough, his first entrance is the not unexpected beginning of such an experience:

Ralph. Come, death, when thou wilt; I am weary of my life!
Merrygreek (to the audience). I told you, I, we should woo another wife!
Ralph. Why did God make me such a goodly person?
Merry. He is in by the week. We shall have sport anon.
Ralph. And where is my trusty friend, Matthew Merrygreek?
Ho! Matthew Merrygreek, a word with thee! . . .
I die except thou help! . . .
Merry. What is it? Has any man threatened you to beat?
Ralph. What is he that durst have put me in'that heat?
He that beateth me—by His arms—shall well find
That I will not be far from him, nor run behind.
Merry. That thing know all men ever since ye overthrew
The fellow of the lion which Hercules 'slew.
But what is it then?
Ralph. Of love I make my moan.

On being told who the woman is, Merrygreek declares:

Yet a fitter wife for your manship might be found.
Such a goodly man as you might get one with land,
Besides pounds of gold a thousand, a thousand,
And a thousand, and a thousand, and a thousand,
And to the sum of twenty-hundred thousand.
Your most goodly personage is worthy of no less.
Ralph. I am sorry God made me so comely, doubtless;
For that maketh me eachwhere so highly favored,
And all women on me so enamored.

> *Merry.* "Enamored," quoth you? Have you spied out that?
> *Ralph.* Yes, eachwhere they gaze all upon me and stare.
> *Merry.* And ye will not believe what they say in the street
> When your maship passeth by, all such as I meet,
> That sometimes I can scarce find what answers to make.
> "Who is this?" saith one, "Sir Launcelot du Lake?"
> "Who is this? Great Guy of Warwick?" saith another.
> "No," say I, "It is the thirteenth Hercules' brother."
> "Who is this? Noble Hector of Troy?" saith the third.
> "No, but of the same nest," say I, "it is a bird."
> "Who is this? Great Goliath, Samson, or Colbrand?"
> "No," say I, "But it is a Brute of the Alie Land."
> "Who is this? Great Alexander, or Charlemagne?"
> "No, it is the Tenth Worthy," say I to them again.
> I know not if I said well.
> > *Ralph.* Yes; for so I am.
> *Merry.* To some others the Third Cato I do you call.
> And so, as well as I can, I answer them all.
> "Sir, I pray you, what lord, or great gentleman, is this?"
> "Master Ralph Roister Doister, dame," say I, iwis.
> "O Lord!" saith she then, "What a goodly man it is;
> Would Christ I had such a husband as he is!" ...
> > *Ralph.* I can thee thank that thou canst such
> Answers devise.
> But I perceive thou dost me throughly know ....
> *Merry.* But now to your widow, whom you love so hot.
> *Ralph.* By Cock! thou sayest truth! I had almost forgot.

The scene is before the house of Christian Custance, the widow about whom Ralph is "so hot." Out come three of the widow's servants, Madge Mumblecrust, the old nurse, with her distaff, Tibet Talkapace, with her sewing, Annot Alyface, with her knitting. Ralph seeks to win the old nurse over to be his go-between in his suit; so he kisses her and whispers in her ear. At this moment Merrygreek, who is mischievously bent on squeezing as much fun out of this ludicrous situation as possible by pretending to believe that Ralph has already won his suit, enters.

> *Merry.* God be at your wedding! Be ye sped already?
> I did not suppose that your love was so greedy.
> I perceive now ye have chose of devotion;

And joy have ye, lady, of your promotion!
   Ralph. Tush, fool, thou art deceived; this is not she.
   Merry. Well, make much of her, and keep her well,
I 'vise ye.
   Margery. What aileth this fellow? He driveth me to weeping.
   Merry. What! weep on the wedding day? Be merry, woman!
Though I say it, ye have chose a good gentleman.
   Ralph. Kock's nowns! what meanest thou, man?
   Merry. Ah, sir, be good to her; she is but a gristle!
Ah! sweet lamb and cony!
   Ralph. Tut, thou art deceived!
   Merry. Weep no more, lady; ye shall be well received.
Up with some merry noise, sirs, to bring home the bride!
   Ralph. Gog's arms, knave! Art thou mad?
I tell thee thou art wide.
   Merry. Then ye intend by night to have her home brought.
   Ralph. I tell thee, no!
   Merry. How then?
   Ralph. 'Tis neither meant nor thought.
   Merry. What shall we then do with her?
   Ralph. Ah, foolish harebrain!
This is not she!
   Merry. No is? Why then, unsaid again.
And what young girl is this with your maship so bold?
   Ralph. A girl?
   Merry. Yes; I dare say scarce yet three score year old.
   Ralph. This same is the fair widow's nurse, of whom ye wot.
   Merry. Is she but a nurse of a house? Hence, home, old trot!
Hence at once!
   Ralph. No! no!
   Merry. What! an please your maship,
A nurse to talk so homely with one of your worship? . . .
   Ralph. She will help forward this my suit.
   Merry. Then is't mine own pigsny, and blessing on my heart

This misunderstanding being thus cleared up, it is decided to
"pipe up a merry note," Ralph's retainers accompanying
themselves in a song, to which the old nurse offers to dance.

    Whoso to marry a minion wife
    Hath had good chance and hap.
    Must love her and cherish her all his life,
    And dandle her in his lap.

If she will fare well, if she will go gay,
A good husband ever still,
Whatever she lust to do or say,
Must let her have her own will.

About what affairs soever he go,
He must show all his mind;
None of his counsel she may be kept fro,
Else is he a man unkind.

The song and dance done, Ralph Roister Doister hands
Madge Mumblecrust, the nurse, a love letter for her mistress:

Ralph. Now, nurse, take this same letter to thy mistress;
And as my trust is in thee, ply my business.
Nurse. It shall be done.
Merry. Who made it?
Ralph. I wrote it, each whit.
Merry. Then needs it no mending.
Ralph. No, no!
Merry. No; I know your wit.

In quick succession the impatient wooer despatches another
emissary with a ring as a token, and has him followed up by
Matthew Merrygreek:

Merry. Dame Custance, God ye save!
Cust. Welcome, friend Merrygreek: and what thing would
ye have?
Merry. I am come to you a little matter to break.
Cust. But see it be honest, else better not to speak.
Merry. How feel ye yourself affected here of late?
Cust. I feel no manner change but after the old rate.
But whereby do you mean?
Merry. Concerning marriage.
Doth not love lade you?
Cust. I feel no such carriage.
Merry. Do ye feel no pangs of dotage? answer me right.
Cust. I dote so that I make but one sleep all the night.
But why need all these words?
Merry. Oh, Jesus! will ye see
What dissembling creatures these same women be?
The gentleman ye wot of, whom you do love

That ye would fain marry him, if ye durst it move,
Among other rich widows, which are of him glad,
Lest ye for losing of him perchance might run mad,
Is now contented that upon your suit making,
Ye be as one in election of taking.
   Cust. What a tale is this! That I wot of? Whom I love?
   Merry. Yea, and he is as loving a worm, again, as a dove.
E'en of very pity he is willing you to take,
Because ye shall not destroy yourself for his sake.
   Cust. Marry, God yield his maship! Whatever he be,
It is gentmanly spoken.
   Merry. Is it not, trow ye?
If ye have the grace now to offer yourself, ye speed.
   Cust. As much as though I did, this time it shall not need.
But what gentman is it, I pray you tell me plain,
That wooeth so finely?
   Merry. Lo where ye be again,
As though ye knew him not!
   Cust. Tush, ye speak in jest!
   Merry. Nay, sure, the party is in good knacking earnest:
And have you he will, he saith, and have you he must . . .
   Cust. He hath no title this way, whatever he be,
Nor I know none to whom I have such word spoken.
   Merry. Ye know him not, you, by his letter and token?
   Cust. Indeed, true it is that a letter I have;
But I never read it yet, as God me save!
   Merry. Ye a woman, and your letter so long unread?
   Cust. Ye may thereby know what haste I have to wed.
But now who it is for my hand, I know by guess.
   Merry. Ah, well I say.
   Cust. It is Roister Doister, doubtless.
   Merry. Will ye never leave this dissimulation?
Ye know him not?
   Cust. But by imagination;
For no man there is but a very dolt and lout
That to woo a widow would so go about
He shall never have me his wife while he do live.
   Merry. Then will he have you, if he may, so mote I thrive!
And he biddeth you send him word by me,
That ye humbly beseech him ye may his wife be,
And that there shall be no let in you, nor mistrust,
But to be wedded on Sunday next, if he lust;
And biddeth you to look for him.
   Cust. Doth he bid so?

Go, say that I bid him keep him warm at home.

When Ralph Roister Doister receives Matthew Merrygreek's report he refuses to live any longer, and lies down to die. Merrygreek calls out Ralph's servants and makes the announcement:

> *Merry.* Come forth, sirs, hear the doleful news
> I shall you tell.
> Our good master here will no longer with us dwell.
> But in spite of Custance which hath him wearied,
> Let us see his maship solemnly buried;
> And while some piece of his soul is yet him within,
> Some part of his funerals let us here begin.

He then proceeds to intone a mock requiem, which he suddenly interrupts as if an idea struck him:

> *Merry.* Soft, hear what I have cast!
> *Ralph.* I will hear nothing; I am passed.
> *Merry.* Ye may tarry one hour, and hear what I shall say.
> Ye were best, sir, for a while to revive again,
> And quit them ere ye go.
> *Ralph.* Trowest thou so?
> *Merry.* Yea, plain.
> *Ralph.* How may I revive, being now so far passed?
> *Merry.* I will rub your temples, and fetch you again at last.
> *Ralph.* It will not be possible.
> *Merry.* Yea, for twenty pound.
> *Ralph.* Arms! What dost thou?
> *Merry.* Fetch you again out of your sound.
> By this cross, ye were nigh gone indeed! I might feel
> Your soul departing within an inch of your heel.
> Now follow my counsel.
> *Ralph.* What is it?
> *Merry.* If I were you,
> Custance should eft seek to me ere I would bow.
> *Ralph.* Well, as thou wilt have me, so will I do.
> *Merry.* Then shall ye revive again for an hour or two?
> *Ralph.* As thou wilt; I am content, for a little space.

He suggests that it might be a good idea for Ralph to speak to the lady himself. To fetch her out they sing the following serenade:

> I mun be married a Sunday,
> I mun be married a Sunday;
> Whosoever shall come that way,
> I mun be married a Sunday.
>
> Roister Doister is my name,
> Roister Doister is my name;
> A lusty brute, I am the same;
> I mun be married a Sunday.
>
> Christian Custance have I found,
> Christian Custance have I found;
> A widow worth a thousand pound.
> I mun be married a Sunday.
>
> Custance is as sweet as honey,
> Custance is as sweet as honey;
> I her lamb and she my coney,
> I mun be married a Sunday.

Dame Custance does come out, but in a fury. She hands Merrygreek the letter Roister Doister had sent her.

> *Cust.* Hold, read it if you can.
> And see what letter it is to win a woman.

And this is what he reads:

> Sweet mistress, whereas I love you nothing at all,
> Regarding your substance and riches chief of all,
> For your personage, beauty, demeanor and wit
> I commend me unto you never a whit.
> Sorry to hear report of your good welfare.
> For (as I hear say) such your conditions are
> That you be worthy favor of no living man. . . .

It goes on in this manner at great length. What has happened, of course, is that the punctuation has been misplaced. The following is the way it was intended to be read:

> Sweet mistress, whereas I love you—nothing at all
> Regarding your riches and substance—chief of all
> For your personage, beauty, demeanor and wit,
> I commend me unto you. Never a whit
> Sorry to hear report of your good welfare;
> For (as I hear say) such your conditions are
> That ye be worthy favor.

It will be remembered that this is the device that Shakespeare employed in the prologue to *Pyramus and Thisbe,* the play-within-the-play in *A Midsummer Night's Dream.* Possibly here is where he got the idea.

The last rejection makes Ralph break down and weep. Merrygreek cheers him up by telling him that he too has something to mourn about.

> *Merry.* I mourn for another thing.
> *Ralph.* What is it, Merrygreek, wherefor thou dost
> grief take?
> *Merry.* That I am not a woman myself for your sake;
> I would have you myself, and a straw for yond Gill!
> And make much of you.
> I would not, I warrant you, fall in such a rage
> As to refuse such a goodly personage.
> *Ralph.* In faith, I heartily thank thee, Merrygreek . . . .
> I dare say thou wouldst have me to thy husband.

And he is comforted. Now Merrygreek recommends resort to force in one final effort. Accordingly, Ralph issues an order to his men:

> Sirs, see that my harness, my target, and my shield
> Be made as bright now as when I was last in field;
> As white as I should to war again tomorrow;
> For sick shall I be but I work some folks sorrow.
> Therefore see that all shine as bright as Saint George. . . .
> I would have my sword and harness to shine so bright
> That I might therewith dim mine enemies' sight.
> And see that in case I should need to come to arming,
> All things may be ready at a minute's warning!
> For such chance may chance in an hour, do you hear?

And sure enough, the "chance" does "chance." Ralph Roister

Doister issues an ultimatum. Dame Custance hurls defiance:
"Ye shall see women's war!" Merrygreek assures Dame Custance
that he has been engineering the farcical courtship for
"pastance"—for the fun of it; and further tells her that in the
coming battle he will pretend to aim blows at her, and manage
to have them land on Ralph.

Both sides marshal their forces—and the battle is joined:

> *Cust.* Maidens, come forth with your tools!
> *Ralph.* In array!
> *Merry.* Dubbadub, sirrah!
> *Ralph.* In array!
> They come suddenly on us!
> *Merry.* Dubbadub!
> *Ralph.* In array!
> That ever I was born! We are taken tardy!
> *Merry.* Now, sirs, quit ourselves like tall men and hardy!
> *Cust.* On afore, Truepenny! Hold thine own, Annot!
> On toward them, Tibet! for 'scape us they cannot.
> Come forth, Madge Mumblecrust! to stand fast togither.
> *Merry.* God send us a fair day!
> *Ralph.* See, they march on hither!
> *Tibet.* But, Mistress!
> *Cust.* What sayest thou?
> *Tibet.* Shall I go fetch the goose?
> *Cust.* What to do?
> *Tibet.* To yonder captain I will turn her loose.
> An she gape and hiss at him, as she does at me,
> I durst jeopard my hand she will make him flee.
> *Cust.* On! Forward!
> *Ralph.* They come!
> *Merry.* Stand!
> *Ralph.* Hold!
> *Merry.* Keep!
> *Ralph.* There!
> *Merry.* Strike!
> *Ralph.* Take heed!
> *Cust.* Well done, Truepenny!
> *True.* Ah, whoreson!
> *Cust.* Well done, indeed!
>
> *Merry.* Hold thine own, Harpax! Down with them, Dobinet!
> *Cust.* Now, Madge! There, Annot! Now stick them, Tibet!
> *Ralph.* They win ground!

Merry. Save yourself, sir, for God's sake!
Ralph. Out, alas! I am slain! Help!
Merry, Save yourself!
Ralph. Alas!
Merry. Nay, then, have at you, mistress!
Ralph. Thou hittest me, alas!
Merry. I will strike at Custance here!
Ralph. Thou hittest me!
Merry. So I will!
Nay, mistress Custance!
Ralph. Alas, thou hittest me still! Hold!
Merry. Save yourself, sir.
Ralph. Help! Out! Alas! I am slain!
Merry. Truce! Hold your hands! Truce for a pissing-while
or twain! . . .
Ralph. Come away! By the matte, she is mankind!
I durst adventure the loss of my right hand
If she did not slay her other husband:
And see, if she prepare not again to fight! . . .
Cust. To it again, my knightesses! Down with them all!
Ralph. Away, away, away! She will else kill us all!
Merry. Nay, stick to it, like a hardy man and tall.
Ralph. Oh, bones! thou hittest me! Away, or else die we shall!
Merry. Away, for the pash of our sweet Lord Jesus Christ!
Cust. Away, lout and lubber! or I shall be thy priest.
(Exeunt Merrygreek, Roister Doister, and his men.)
Cust. So this field is ours; we have driven them all away.
Now Roister Doister will no more wooing begin.

The last act introduces an element of suspense. Gawyn Goodluck, to whom Christian Custance is engaged to be married, returns from his travels and hears disquieting rumors about his sweetheart's involvement with Ralph Roister Doister. The tragic mood does not last long, however. The difficulty is easily cleared up, and Gawyn Goodluck, regretting the unhappiness which his suspicious attitude has in the meanwhile caused Dame Custance, announces:

Well, now to make you for this some part of amends,
I shall desire first you, and then such of our friends
As shall to you seem best, to sup at home with me,
Where at your fought field we shall laugh and merry be.

Included among the guests, on Goodluck's insistence, is Ralph Roister Doister.

The play closes with the traditional prayer for the reigning monarch—in this case, Queen Mary.

In the Prologue to *Ralph Roister Doister* Udall informs us that mirth is good for the health, and that he is going to supply it. But he does not say that that is the reason why he wrote the play. The purpose of the play, he says, is to castigate the vice of braggadocio:

> Our comedy or interlude which we intend to play
> Is named *Roister Doister* indeed,
> Which against the vain-glorious doth inveigh
> Whose humor the roisting sort continually doth feed.

However, when we are through with the play we cannot remember where he does "inveigh" against the vice. The medieval tradition, which made art the handmaid of religion or morality, was still potent enough to make him, particularly as a pedagogue, conscious of what was expected of him.

On the other hand, the author of *Gammer Gurton's Needle* was completely liberated from the dictates of the Middle Ages. If there is any instruction in the play it is of the kind embodied in the following song:

> Back and side go bare, go bare,
> Both foot and hand go cold;
> But belly, God send thee good ale enough,
> Whether it be new or old.
> I cannot eat but little meat,
> My stomach is not good;
> But sure I think that I could drink
> With him that wears a hood.
> Though I go bare, take ye no care,
> I am nothing acold;
> I stuff my skin so full within
> Of jolly good ale and old.
> Back and side go bare, go bare, &c.
>
> I love no roast but a nut brown toast,
> And a crab laid in the fire.

A little bread shall do me stead,
Much bread I not desire.
No frost, nor snow, no wind, I trow,
Can hurt me if I wold;
I am so wrapped, and throughly lapped
Of jolly good ale and old.
Back and side go bare, go bare, &c.

And Tib my wife, that as her life
Loveth well good ale to seek,
Full oft drinks she till ye may see
The tears run down her cheek;
Then doth she troll to me the bowl,
Even as a malt-worm should,
And saith, sweetheart, I took my part
Of this jolly good ale and old.
Back and side, go bare, &c.

Now let them drink till they nod and wink,
Even as good fellows should do;
They shall not miss to have the bliss
Good ale doth bring them to;
And all poor souls that have scoured bowls,
Or have them lustly trolled,
God save the lives of them and their wives,
Whether they be young or old.
Back and side go bare, &c.

The whole play is as native English as the song is. It owes nothing to Plautus or Terence—unless it be the five act structure, and that indebtedness is shared by the entire Elizabethan drama. In Schelling's words, "It is in bustling, vulgar *Gammer Gurton* that we find for the first time a budded sapling of genuine English growth." Even the language is dialectic English.

Gammer Gurton's Needle must be accounted a better play than *Ralph Roister Doister,* good as that is. The handling of the verse is more mature: the substance and form of the line are less frequently determined by the exigencies of the rhyme. The characters in the latter are admirably sketched, which is all that is demanded by the farcical nature of the story. In the former they are well rounded personalities, actors in domestic comedy reflecting life in an English village, even though what sparks the action is the trivial, the farcical, event of the loss of a needle (*neele* in the local dialect).   With delightful humor the author magnifies the trivial event to momentous importance.

The parasite of Plautus is transformed into the itinerant mischief maker, Diccon the Bedlam. He comes into the village and is puzzled by the unwonted gloom that has settled over Gammer Gurton's house:

> There is howling and scowling, all cast in a dump,
> With whewling and puling, as though they had lost a trump.
> Sighing and sobbing, they weep and they wail;
> I marvel in my mind what the devil they ail.
> The old trot sits groaning, with "alas!" and "alas!"
> And Tib wrings her hands, and takes on in worse case. . . .
> I fear me the folks be not well in their wits.
> Ask them what they ail, or who brought them in this stay,
> They answer not at all, but "alack!" and "wellaway!"

He asks Hodge, the farm-hand, what has happened; but Hodge doesn't know. Hodge then asks Tib, the maid:

> I say, Tib—if thou be Tib, as I trow sure thou be—
> What devil make ado is this, between our dame and thee?
>   *Tib.* Gog's head, Hodge, thou had a good turn thou wert
>   not here this while!
> It had been better for some of us to have been hence a mile;
> My grammer is so out of course and frantic all at once,
> That Cock, our boy, and I, poor wench,
> Have felt it on our bones.
>   *Hodge.* What is the matter—say on, Tib—Whereof
>   she taketh so on?
>   *Tib.* She is undone, she saith, alas! Her joy and life is gone!
> If she hear not of some comfort, she is, faith! but dead.
>   *Hodge.* By'r Lady, cham [I am] not very glad to see her in
>   this dump.
> Chold [I hold] a noble her stool hath fallen, and she hath
>   broke her rump.
>   *Tib.* Nay, and that were the worst, we would not greatly
>   care
> For bursting of her buckle-bone, or breaking of her chair;
> But greater, greater, is her grief, as, Hodge, we shall all feel!

> *Hodge.* Gog's wounds, Tib! my gammer has never lost her neele?
> *Tib.* Her neele!
> *Hodge.* Her neele!
> *Tib.* Her neele!
> By Him that made me, it is true, Hodge, I tell thee.

The bad news is confirmed by Gammer Gurton herself:

> Alas, Hodge, alas! I may well curse and ban
> This day that ever I saw it, with Gib and the milk-pan;
> For these and ill luck together, as knoweth Cock, my boy,
> Have struck away my dear neele, and robbed me of my joy,
> My fair long straight neele, that was mine only treasure!
>   *Hodge.* Might ha kept it when ye had it! but fools will
>   be fools still . . .
>   *Hodge.* Here is a pretty matter, to see this gear how it goes.
> By Gog's soul, I think you would lose your arse
>   and it were loose! . . .
> Gog's death! how shall my breeches be sewed? Shall I go
>   thus tomorrow?
> Whereto served your hands and eyes, but this your neele
>   to keep?
> What devil had you else to do?
> Cham [I am] fain abroad to dig and delve in water,
>   mire and clay,
> Sossing and possing in the dirt still from day to day.
> A hundred things that be abroad cham set to see them weele,
> And four of you sit idle at home and cannot keep a neele!

We presently realize why Hodge is so unreasonably offensive, when he explains to Diccon the Bedlam the reason why he is so upset about his breeches not being decently patched:

> Kirstian Clack, Tim Simpson's maid, comes hither tomorrow.
> Cham not able to say between us what may hap;
> She smiled on me the last Sunday, when ich put off my cap.

It dawns upon Diccon that the loss of Gammer Gurton's needle afforded him a splendid opportunity for mischief:

> Here is a matter of worthy glosing,
> Of Gammer Gurton's needle losing . . .

> A man I think could make a play,
> And need no wurd to this they say,
> Being but half a clark.

In other words, a man lacking literary ability could make a play out of material offered, by merely writing down verbatim what the people involved actually say—an interesting lesson in realistic drama. He turns to the audience:

> Soft, let me alone! I will take the charge
> This matter further to enlarge . . . .
> If ye will mark my toys, and note,
> I will give ye leave to cut my throat
> If I make not a good sport.

He promptly proceeds to make the first move. He walks over to Gammer Gurton's neighbor, Dame Chat, who greets him cordially, and invites him in to join in a card game. He declines, telling her that he has a matter of importance to impart to her in private, if she solemnly promises to keep it secret.

> *Chat.* Gog's bread! that will I do!
> As secret as mine own thought, by God and the devil too!
>   *Diccon.* Here is Gammer Gurton, your neighbor, a sad
>   and heavy wight.
> Her godly fair red cock at home was stole this last night.
>   *Chat.* Gog's soul! Her cock with the yellow legs that
>   nightly crowed so just?
>   *Diccon.* That cock is stolen.
>   *Chat.* What, was he fetched out of the hen's roost?
>   *Diccon.* I cannot tell where the devil he was kept,
> But Tib hath tickled in Gammer's ear that you should steal
>   the cock.
>   *Chat.* Have I! strong whore? by bread and salt!—
>   *Diccon.* What soft, I say, be still!
> Say not one word for all this gear.
>   *Chat.* By the Mass, that I will!
> I will have the young whore by the head, and the old trot
>   by the throat.
>   *Diccon.* Not one word, Dame Chat! I say; not one word!
>   *Chat.* Shall such a begger's brawl as that, thinkest thou,
>   make me a thief?
> The pox light on her whore's sides, a pestilence and a mischief!

> Come out, thou hungry needy bitch!
> O that my nails be short!
>   *Diccon.* Gog's bread, woman, hold your peace! . . .
> Did ye not swear ye would be ruled, before the tale I told? . . .
>   *Chat.* Would you suffer, yourself, Diccon, such a sort
>   to revile you,
> With slanderous words to blot your name, and to defile you?
>   *Diccon.* No, Goodwife Chat, I would be loth such drabs
>   should blot my name;
> But yet ye must so order all that Diccon bear no blame.

So much for move number one. Diccon has suitably conditioned Dame Chat for an encounter with Gammer Gurton. His next move must be to condition Gammer Gurton for that encounter. Accordingly, he prepares the audience for his visit to that lady:

> Ye see, masters that one end tapped, of this my short advice.
> Now must we broach th'other too, before the smoke arise;
> And by the time they have awhile run, I trust ye need not
>   crave it;
> But look, what lieth in both their hearts ye are like,
>   sure, to have it.

He comes upon Gammer Gurton while she is still bemoaning the loss of her precious needle.

> *Gammer.* Good Lord, shall never by my luck my neele
>   again to spy?
> Alas, the while! 'tis past my help; where 'tis still it must lie!
>   *Diccon.* Now, Jesus! Gammer Gurton, what driveth you
>   to this sadness? . . .
> *Gammer.* Who is that? What, Diccon? Cham lost, man!
>   fie, fie!
> *Diccon.* Marry, fie on them that be worthy. But what
>   should be your trouble?
> *Gammer.* Alas! the more ich think on it, my sorrow it
>   waxeth double.
> My goodly tossing spurriers neele chave lost, ich wot not where.
>   *Diccon.* Your neele? When?
> *Gammer.* My neele, alas! ich might full ill it spare . . .
>   *Diccon.* If this be all, good Gammer, I warrant you all
>   is save.
> *Gammer.* Why, know you any tidings which way my

neele is gone?

Diccon. Yea, that I do doubtless, as ye shall hear anon.
A see a thing this matter toucheth, within these twenty hours,
Even at this gate, before my face, by a neighbor of yours.
She stooped me down, and up she took a needle or a pin.
I durst be sworn it was even yours, by all my mother's kin.

Gammer. It was my neele, Diccon, ich wot: for here,
even by this post.

Ich sat what time as ich upstart, and so my neele it lost.
Who was it, lief son? Speak, ich pray thee, and quickly
tell me that!

Diccon. A subtle quean as any in this town, your
neighbor here, Dame Chat.

Gammer. Dame Chat, Diccon? Let me be gone; chill
thither in post haste . . .

Thinks the false quean by such a slight that chill my
neele lack?

Diccon. Sleep not your gear, I counsel you: but of this
take good heed;

Let not be known I told you of it, how well soever ye speed.
(Exit Gammer.)

Diccon. (To the audience.) Here will the sport begin;
if these two once may meet,

Their cheer, durst lay money, will prove scarcely sweet . . . .
He that may tarry by it awhile, and that but short,
I warrant him, trust to it, he shall see all the sport.

In the ensuing altercation and struggle the needle is never
mentioned, Dame Chat assuming that Gammer Gurton has
come to claim her cock. The battle ends with Dame Chat
throwing Gammer Gurton to the ground and escaping into her
house. Gammer Gurton decides that the best thing to do is to
send for Doctor Rat, the parson, to help her:

Gammer. We have a parson, Hodge, thou knowest, a man
esteemed wise.

Mast Doctor Rat; chill for him send, and let me hear his advice.
He will her shrive for all this gear, and give her penance strait;
Wese have our neele, else Dame Chat comes ne'er within
heaven gate.

Dr. Rat is summoned, and, characteristically, arrives grum-
bling.

A man were better twenty times be a bandog and bark,
Than here among such a sort to be parish priest or clark,
Where he shall never be at rest one pissing-while a day,
But he must trudge about the town, this way and that way;
Here to drab, there to thief, his shoes to rent . . .
And which is worst of all, at every knave's commandment!
I had not sit the space to drink two pots of ale,
But Gammer Gurton's sorry boy was straightway at my tail;
And she was sick, and I must come, to do I wot not what!
If once her finger's end but ache, trudge! Call for Doctor Rat!
And when I come not at their call, I only thereby lose;
For I am sure to lack therefore a tithe pig or a goose.
I warrant you, when truth is known and told they have
   their tale.
The matter whereabout I come is not worth a halfpenny
   worth of ale.
Yet must I talk so sage and smooth as though I were a glozer;
Else, ere the year come at an end I shall be sure the loser.

When he meets Gammer Gurton his tone changes instantly:

What work ye, Gammer Gurton? How? Here is your friend
   Mast Rat.
   Gammer. Ah, good Mast Doctor! Cha troubled, cha
   troubled you . . . .
   Rat. How do ye, woman? Be ye lusty, or be ye not
   well at ease?
   Gammer. By gis, Master, cham not sick, but yet
   chave a disease.
Chad a foul turn now of late.
      Rat. Hath your brown cow cast her calf, or
   your sandy sow her pigs?
   Gammer. No, but chad been as good they had as this.
   Rat. What is the matter?
   Gammer. Alas, alas! cha lost my good neele!
My neele, I say; and wot ye what? a drab came by and
   spied it.
And when I asked her for the same, the filth flatly
   denied it.
   Rat. What was she that?
   Gammer. A dame, ich warrant you! She began to scold
   and brawl—
Alas, alas! Come hither, Hodge! This wretch can tell you all.

And the slow-witted Hodge proceeds to tell the story:

> My Gammer Gurton here, see now,
>   sat down at this door, see now;
> And as she began to stir her, see now,
>   her neele fell to the floor, see now;
> And while her staff she took, see now,
>   at Gib, her cat, to fling, see now . . .

He thus proceeds for twenty-four lines, each line ending in "see now."

> *Rat.* What would you have me to do?
> I will do the best that I can do, to set you both at one.
> But be ye sure Dame Chat hath this your neele found?

At this point Diccon enters. He does not deny the story he told, but he refused to have it established that he was the tale bearer. However, he assures his innocent dupes that if he now pays a visit to Dame Chat he is sure to get results: he does not tell them what results. That he confides in the audience:

> Now, sirs, do ye no more but keep my counsel just,
> And Doctor Rat shall thus catch some good, I trust.
> But Mother Chat, my gossip, talk first withal I must:
> For she must be chief captain to lay the rat in the dust.

If Doctor Rat has involved himself in this mischievous game, he plans to make him share the consequences. How to accomplish this he does not yet know; but when, in his interview with Dame Chat she brags how well she had acquitted herself in the recent battle against Gammer Gurton and Hodge, he conceives an idea. He informs her that Hodge intends to get revenge by creeping into her house through a certain hole in the wall and killing all her hens. He advises her to be properly prepared for him. We understand, of course, that the trap is being set, not for Hodge, but for Dr. Rat.

He reports to Dr. Rat that he has seen Dame Chat sewing with the needle, and tells him that if he follows his directions he will catch Dame Chat red-handed, with the needle in her hand:

> *Rat.* For God's sake, do so, Diccon, and I will 'gage
> my gown

To give thee a full pot of the best ale in town.
    Diccon. Follow me but a little, and mark what I will say; . . .
See ye not what is here? A hole where in ye may creep
Into the house, and suddenly unawares among them leap.
There shall ye find the bitchfox and the neele together. . .
    Rat. Art thou sure, Diccon, the swill-tub stands not
    hereabout?
    Diccon. I was within myself, man, even now; there is
    no doubt.
Go softly, make no noise; give me your foot, Sir John.
Here will I wait upon you, till you come out anon.

Inside the women fall upon him, taking him to be Hodge.

    Rat. Help, Diccon! Out! alas! I shall be slain among them!
    Diccon. If they give you not the needle, tell them that
    ye will hang them!
'Ware that! How, my wenches! Have ye caught the fox
That used to make revel among your hens and cocks?
Save his life yet for his order, though he sustain some pain.
Gog's bread! I am afraid they will beat out his brain.

Dr. Rat vows to go to law, and has the bailiff, Master Bayly, summoned. He is a sensible man, and listens carefully to the story the parson has to tell.

    Bayley. I can perceive none other, I speak it from my heart,
But either ye are in all the fault, or else in the greatest part.
    Rat. If it be counted his fault besides all his grieves,
When a poor man is spoiled and beaten among thieves,
Then I confess my fault herein, at this season;
But I hope you will not judge so much against reason.
    Bayley. And, methinks, by your own tale, of all that
    ye name,
If any played the thief, you were the very same.
The women they did nothing, as your words make probation,
But stoutly withstood your forcible invasion.
If that a thief at your window to enter should begin,
Would you hold forth your hand to help to pull him in?
Or would you keep him out? I pray you answer me.
    Rat. Marry, keep him out, and a good cause why.
But I am no thief, sir, but an honest learned clark.
    Bayly. Yea, but who knoweth that when he meets

you in the dark?
I am sure your learning shines not out at your nose!
Was it any marvel though the poor woman arose
And start up, being afraid of that was in her purse?
Methinks you may be glad that your luck was no worse.
 Rat. Is not this evil enough, I pray you think?
  (Showing his broken head.)
 Bayly. Yea, but a man in the dark, if chances do wink,
As soon he smites his father as any other man,
Because of lack of light descern him he ne can.
Might it not have been your luck with a spit to have
 been slain? . . .
 Rat. Well, will you be so good, sir, as talk with Dame Chat,
And know what she intended? I ask no more than that.
 Bayly. Let her be called. .
I warrant in this case she will be her own proctor;
She will tell her own tale, in metre or in prose,
And bid you seek your remedy, and so go wipe your nose.

Dame Chat is summoned; and is told that she is accused by Dr.
Rat of attempting to murder him:

 Chat. That I would have murdered him? Fie on him, wretch.
I will swear on all the books that opens and shuts,
He feigneth this tale out of his own guts;
For this seven weeks with me I am sure he sat not down . . .
What, man, will you say I broke your head?
 Rat. How canst thou prove the contrary?
 Chat. Nay, how provest thou that I did the deed?
 Rat. Too plainly, by St. Mary:
This proof, I trow, may serve, though I no word spoke.
  (Showing his broken head.)
 Chat. Because thy head is broken, was it I that it broke?
I saw thee, Rat, I tell thee, not once within this fortnight.
 Rat. No, marry, thou sawest me not, for why thou hadst
no light . . . .
 Bayly. Answer me to this, Mast Rat: when caught you
this harm of yours?
 Rat. A while ago, sir, God he knoweth, within less than
these two hours.
 Bayly. Dame Chat, was there none with you (confess,
i'faith) about that season?

What, woman? Let it be what it will, 'tis neither felony nor
    treason.
    Chat. Yea, by my faith, Master Bayly, there was a knave
    not far
Who caught one good fillip on the brow with a door-bar,
And well was he worthy, as it seemed to me.
But what is that to this man, since this was not he?
    Bayly. Who was it then? let's hear!
    Rat. Alas, sir, ask you that?
Is it not made plain enough by the own mouth of
    Dame Chat?
The time agreeth, my head is broken, her tongue cannot lie;
Only upon a bare nay she says it was not I.
    Chat. No, marry, was it not indeed! . . . .
    Bayly. Yet tells thou not who it was.
    Chat. Who it was? A false thief,
That came like a false fox my pullain to kill and mischief!
    Bayly. But knowest thou not his name?
    Chat. I know it; but what then?
It was that crafty cullion, Hodge, my Gammer Gurton's man.

Hodge is called but, of course, reveals no sign of head injury; so
the bailiff has to proceed with the cross examination. In a scene
developed with the skill of a master dramatist, Diccon emerges
as the prime mover in the series of mystifying situations.

Mr. Bayly rather enjoys the joke, and is inclined to be
indulgent when he questions Diccon; who, in his turn, remains
saucy:

    Bayly. Diccon, here be two or three thy company cannot
    spare.
    Diccon. God bless you, an you may be blest, so many
    all at once!
    Chat. Come knave, it were a good deed to geld thee,
    by Cock's bones!
Seest not thy handiwork? Sir Rat, can ye forbear him?
    Diccon. A vengeance on those hands light, for my hands
    came not near him.
The whoreson priest hath lift the pot in some of these
    alewives' chairs,
That his head would not serve him, belike, to come down
    the stairs

Bayly. Nay, soft! Thou mayest not play the knave,
and have this language too!
If thou thy tongue bridle a while, she better mayest thou do.
Confess the truth, as I shall ask, and cease awhile to fable;
And for thy fault I promise thee thy handling shall be
reasonable.
Hast thou not made a lie or two, to set these two by the ears?
    Diccon. What if I have? Five hundred such have I seen
within these seven years:
I am sorry for nothing else but that I see not the sport
Which was between them when they met, as they
themselves report.
    Bayly. The greatest thing—Master Rat, ye see how he
is drest!
    Diccon. What devil need he be groping so deep in
Goodwife Chat's hens' nest?
    Bayly. Yea, but it was thy drift to bring him into the briars.
    Diccon. God's bread! Hath not such an old fool wit
to save his ears? . . .
    Rat. In the king's name, Master Bayly, I charge you
set him fast.
    Diccon. What, fast at cards, or fast on sleep? It is the thing
I did last.
    Rat. Nay, fast in fetters, false varlet, according to
thy deeds
    Bayly. Master Doctor, there is no remedy; I must entreat
you needs
Some other kind of punishment.
    Rat. Nay, by all hallows,
His punishment, if I may judge, shall be naught else
but the gallows.
    Bayly. That were too sore; a spiritual man to be so
extreme!

The whole group become infected with the bailiff's good
humor, and everyone agrees to accept his verdict. And this is
the penalty he imposes upon Diccon:

To recompense this thy former action—
Because thou has offended all, to make them satisfaction,
Before their faces here kneel down, and, as I shall thee teach—
For thou shalt take an oath of Hodge's leather breech:
First, for Master Doctor: upon pain of his curse,

Where he will pay for all, thou never draw thy purse;
And when ye meet at one pot he shall have the first pull,
And thou shalt never offer him the cup but it be full.
To Goodwife Chat thou shalt be sworn, even on the same
    wise,
If she refuse thy money once, never to offer it twice.
Thou shalt be bound by the same, here as thou dost take it,
When thou mayest drink of free cost, thou never forsake it.
For Gammer Gurton's sake, again sworn shalt thou be,
To help her to her needle again if it do lie in thee . . .
Last of all, for Hodge the oath to scan,
Thou shalt never take him for fine gentleman.
    Hodge. (On his knees). Come, on, fellow Diccon, chall
    be even with thee now!
    Bayly. Thou wilt not stick to do this, Diccon, I trow?
    Diccon. Now, by my father's skin! My hand down I lay it!
Look, as I have promised, I will not denay it.

Instead of laying his hand down gently on Hodge's buttock, he gives it a resounding slap, which evokes a shriek from Hodge:

Gog's heart! thou false villain, dost thou bite me?

    Bayly. What, Hodge, doth he hurt thee ere ever he begin?
    Hodge. He thrust me into the buttock with a bodkin
    or a pin!
(Feeling his buttock) I say, Gammer! Gammer!
    Gammer. How now, Hodge, how now?
    Hodge. God's malt, Gammer Gurton!
    Gammer. Thou art mad, ich trow!
    Hodge. Will you see the devil, Gammer?
    Gammer. The devil, son? God bless us!
    Hodge. Chould ich were hanged, Gammer—
    Gammer. Marry, see, ye might dress us—
    Hodge. Chave it, by the mass, Gammer!
    Gammer. What? Not my neele, Hodge?
    Hodge. Your neele, Gammer! your neele!
    Gammer. No, fie, thou dost but dodge!
    Hodge. Cha found your neele, Gammer, Here in my
    hand be it!
    Gammer. For all the loves on earth, Hodge, let me see it!
    Hodge. Soft, Gammer!
    Gammer. Good Hodge!
    Hodge. Soft, ich say; tarry awhile!

> *Gammer.* Nay, sweet Hodge, say truth, and do not
> me beguile!
> *Hodge.* Cham sure on it, ich warrant you; it goes no
> more astray.
> *Gammer.* Hodge, when I speak so fair, wilt still say
> me nay?
> *Hodge.* Go near the light, Gammer; this—well, in faith,
> good luck!
> Chwas almost undone, 'twas so far in my buttock!
> *Gammer.* 'Tis mine own dear neele, Hodge, sickerly I wot!

So Diccon did help Gammer Gurton to recover her precious needle, though not in a manner expected. The play ends in general rejoicing, with the entire company, at Gammer Gurton's invitation, entering Dame Chat's establishment to partake of her good ale. Diccon has the last word, addressed to the audience:

> Since at our last ending thus merry we be,
> For Gammer Gurton's Needle's sake, let us have a *Plaudite.*

The closing couplet forcibly suggests a performance by professional actors before the general public. If the title page of the earliest extant edition, that of 1575, did not tell us that this "Ryght Pithy, pleasant and merie Comedie: Intytuled Gammer Gurtons Needle" had been "Played on Stage not longe ago in Christes College in Cambridge," (which, by the way, does not prove that it was *originally* acted there) it would never occur to us that the play had any connection with the academic world.

It has seemed advisable to treat these two plays in this order, as better illustrating the transition from the past to the future in the development of the English drama. *Ralph Roister Doister* still has links with the past: *Gammer Gurton's Needle* has none. Yet chronologically the latter claims precedence. The lengthy prayer for the queen at the end of the former places it after the accession of Mary in that year; while Dr. Rat's demand that Diccon be arrested "in the king's name" places the latter before the death of Edward VI in that year. The following statement by Professor Schelling will therefore serve as an appropriate summing up and appraisal: "It is in bustling, vulgar *Gammer Gurton* that we find for the first time a budded sapling of genuine English growth. This realistic picture of the flurried

Gammer, her dullard man, Hodge, the shameless mischief-monger, Diccon of Bedlam, and a hamlet topsy-turvy over the loss of a needle, may well stand forth *par excellence* as the earliest regular English play."

VI. THE INNS OF COURT 1

In Chapter IV, we considered a group of plays that were the product of a literary circle whose central figure was the great Sir Thomas More, two other prominent members being More's brother-in-law, John Rastell, and Rastell's son-in-law, John Heywood. We found some of the plays to be not at all bad. The production of these plays in the first quarter of the sixteenth century would justify the assumption that the modern English drama had now got off to a good start, and that its future from here on was merely a matter of natural development. But that development was unfortunately arrested. The coming of the Reformation to England plunged the country into a religious conflict which destroyed the possibility of healthy artistic creation, for which national unity is a necessary condition. All three of the important figures in our literary coterie became involved in the conflict. More and Rastell were both thrown into prison. More was executed, but Rastell cheated the block by dying in confinement. John Heywood died in exile. That's the story of three promising playwrights. The national unity essential for healthy artistic creation did not return until the accession of Elizabeth. Then a fresh start had to be made.

Among the institutions that fostered the drama after the accession of Elizabeth were the Inns of Court. The Inns of Court were the law schools of England. Law was a highly respected profession, and its followers, including the students, felt themselves able and duty-bound to help determine national policy. Accordingly, the students of the Inner Temple, one of the Inns of Court, proceeded to teach the young Queen a lesson in the conduct of affairs. In view of existing conditions they felt called upon to stress three points: first, that she must beware of flattering young courtiers and give ear only to grave counselors; second, that she must suppress any disaffection among the masses with a ruthless hand; third, and most important, that she must marry, in order to insure a definite succession to the throne. They thought the best way to teach the lesson was to present before the Queen a play that enacted a horrible example. In this way was born what is known as the first regular tragedy in the English language; namely, *Gorboduc,* presented before Queen Elizabeth during the Christmas season of 1561-62. It was written by two students, Thomas Sackville and Thomas Norton, both of whom later became distinguished members of the parliament that was so insistent that the Queen marry.

To drive their lesson home the more effectively they drew the material of their plot from legendary British history. Garboduc is a legendary king of Britain, who, like King Lear, against the advice of his Counselors, decides to retire, and divides his kingdom between his two sons, Ferrex and Porrex. As was to be expected, trouble begins at once. Ferrex, the elder brother, feels that he has been unwarrantably deprived of half the kingdom. And there is not wanting a parasitic courtier to encourage him in his dissatisfaction. In fact, he advises him to prove his desert by waging war against his brother and slaying him, thus getting possession of the kingdom to which he was entitled.

Ferrex repels the sinister advice. But it occurs to him that there may be a counselor at the court of his brother giving him similar advice. Unwilling to be caught napping, he determines to embark on a policy of secret preparedness. Of course, the secret preparations could not remain secret, and Porrex, hearing of them, decides to strike first. An appeal is made to the old retired king to intercede. But it is too late. A messenger arrives with the report that Porrex has invaded his brother's domain and killed him. Porrex appears before his father and begs forgiveness, but is repulsed. Presently, we are informed that he has been stabbed to the heart by his mother. To avenge the foul deed, the people rise in rebellion and slay both the king and the queen. The uprising is quelled with great slaughter; but one of the nobles, who is called the Duke of Albany, but is spoken of persistently as a foreigner, taking advantage of the fact that the kingdom is left without an heir, decides to make a try for the throne. He is announced approaching with an army of 20,000, and the play ends with the prospect of more slaughter.

Sounds crude, and reeks with blood; yet, if skeletons alone were considered, would it fare so badly in comparison with *Hamlet,* say? The Tragedy of Blood is the name given to a type that was popular in the Elizabethan Age; and the first English tragedy belongs to this type.

When one reads the story of this play, one gets the impression that there is much activity on the stage. But the fact is that there is nothing doing. It is all talk and no action. All the action is supposed to take place behind the scenes and is reported by a messenger, as in the ancient Greek and Roman drama. And *Gorboduc* is patterned after the Roman tragedies ascribed to Seneca. This fact does not surprise us when we realize that the play was written by students. What is noteworthy is the way the play *departs* from ancient practice. In the ancient drama there was no change of place, and no lapse of time. The action could not cover more than one day. These requirements, which were known as the Unities of Place and Time, were strenuously insisted on by the Renaissance critics. Yet this play, which was written by students under academic influence, and for a highly select audience of the cultured, ignores those unities, and adopts the practice which was traditional in English dramatic activity from the days of the miracle plays, when Noah could pause for a few moments, and then say: "Now forty days have fully passed." Nothing could more adequately demonstrate the potency of that traditional practice. A fortunate thing for the English drama; for, as already pointed out, those countries in which the ancient rules prevailed failed to produce a truly great drama.

Another characteristic of *Gorboduc* that we must not overlook is its metrical construction. It is written in blank verse, the prevailing meter employed by Shakespeare and his contemporaries. Those two young men, Sackville and Norton, certainly were enterprising. They did not invent blank verse, but they were the first to use it for a play. Thus the first English tragedy is also the first tragedy written in blank verse. The verse may be stiff, but it is a beginning.

Let us consider a few specimens, which will enable us, at the same time, to see with what effectiveness the authors presented the three main points in their lesson. First, the matter of the advisers. Dordan, the old Counselor, assigned to the elder son, writes to the father:

> My lord Ferrex, your eldest son, misled
> By traitorous fraud of young untempered wits,
> Assembled force against your younger son,
> Ne can my counsel yet withdraw the heat

> And furious pangs of his inflamed head.

And in the midst of the chaos at the end, Eubulus, the old King's Counselor, ruefully observes:

> Hereto it comes when kings will not consent
> To grave advice, but follow willful will.

Now for the second point: the necessity for an iron hand in dealing with the masses who dare make active objection to the deeds of royalty, even when royalty is admittedly wrong:

> *Guenard.* Shall subjects dare with force
> To work revenge upon their prince's fact?
> Admit the worst that may,-as sure in this
> The deed was foul, the queen to slay her son,
> Shall yet the subject seek to take the sword,
> Arise against his lord, and slay his king?
> O wretched state, where those rebellious hearts
> Are not rent out even from their living breasts,
> And with the body thrown unto the fouls
> As carrion food, for terror of the rest.
> *Fergus.* There can no punishment be thought too great
> For this so grievous crime.
> *Eubulus.* We all, my lords, I see, consent in one,
> And I as one consent with ye all in all.
> I hold it more than need, with sharpest law
> To punish this tumultuous bloody rage.
> For nothing more can shake the common state
> Than sufferance of uproars without redress. . . .
> Eke fully with the duke my mind agrees,
> That no cause serves whereby the subject may
> Call to account the doings of his prince,
> Much less in blood by sword to work revenge,
> No more than may the hand cut off the head.
> In act nor speech, no, not in secret thought,
> The subject may rebel against his lord,
> Or judge of him that sits in Caesar's seat . . . .
> Though kings forget to govern as they ought,
> Yet subjects must obey as they are bound.

Could the principle of divine right go any further? The fact is that seven of the last nine lines were suppressed in the authorized edition of the play—suppressed, in all likelihood, by Norton, who was a Puritan. Sackville was the aristocrat. He became Lord Buckhurst.

Further on, Eubulus expresses this opinion of the common people:

> For, give once sway to the people's lusts
> To rush forth on, and stay them not in time,
> And as the stream that rolleth down the hill,
> So will they headlong run with raging thoughts
> From blood to blood, from mischief unto moe,
> To ruin of the realm, themselves, and all,—
> So giddy are the common people's minds,
> So glad of change, more wavering than the sea.

Finally, for the third, and most important, point: the necessity for Queen Elizabeth to marry, in order to insure a definite succession to the throne. What a dismal prospect if there is no heir to the throne is painted by Eubulus at the end of the tragedy:

> Lo, here the end of Brutus' royal line,
> And lo, the entry to the woeful wrack
> And utter ruin of this noble realm!
> The royal king and eke his sons are slain;
> No ruler rests within the regal seat,
> The heir to whom the sceptre 'longs, unknown;
> That to each force of foreign princes' power
> Whom vantage of our wretched state may move
> By sudden arms to gain so rich a realm,
> And to the proud and greedy mind at home
> Whom blinded lust to reign leads to aspire,
> Lo, Britain realm is left an open prey,
> A present spoil by conquest to ensue.
> Who seeth not now how many rising minds
> Do feed their thought with hope to reach a realm?
> And who will not by force attempt to win
> So great a gain, that hope persuades to have?
> A simple color will for title serve:
> Who wins the royal crown will want no right,
> Nor such as shall display by long descent
> A lineal race to prove him lawful king.

In the meanwhile these civil arms shall rage,
And thus a thousand mischiefs shall unfold,
And far and near spread thee, O Britain Land!
All right and law shall cease; and he that had
Nothing today, tomorrow shall enjoy
Great heaps of gold, and he that flowed in wealth,
Lo, he shall be bereft of life and all;
And happiest he that then possesseth least.
The wives shall suffer rape, the maids deflowered,
And the children fatherless shall weep and wail.
With fire and sword thy native folk shall perish;
One kinsman shall bereave another's life;
The father shall unwitting slay the son,
The son shall slay the sire and know it not.
Women and maids the cruel soldier's sword
Shall pierce to death, and silly children, lo,
That playing in the streets and fields are found,
By violent hand shall close their latter day.
Whom shall the fierce and bloody soldier
Reserve to life? Whom shall he spare from death?
Even thou, O wretched mother, half alive,
Thou shalt behold thy dear and only child
Slain with the sword while he yet sucks thy breast.
Lo, guiltless blood shall thus each-where be shed.
Thus shall the wasted soil yield forth no fruit.
But dearth and famine shall possess the land.
The towns shall be consumed and burnt with fire,
The peopled cities shall wax desolate;
And thou, O Britain, whilom in renown,
Whilom in wealth and fame, shall thus be torn,
Dismembered thus, and thus be rent in twain,
Thus wasted and defaced, spoiled and destroyed.
These be the fruits your civil wars will bring.
Hereto it comes when kings will not consent
To grave advice, but follow willful will . . .
And this doth grow when, lo, unto the prince
Whom death or sudden hap of life bereaves,
No certain heir remains.

A dismal prospect indeed! Yet it did not suffice to induce the Queen to marry. She ignored the "grave advice" and remained England's Virgin Queen.

It would be unreasonable to suppose that Shakespeare was

not familiar with this play. He probably had Eubulus's speech in mind when, in *Henry the Sixth,* he depicted the appalling consequences of the conflict between rival claimants to the crown. He even included the episodes of the father unknowingly killing his son, and the son similarly killing his father.

VII. THE INNS OF COURT 2

The tragedy *Gorboduc* was composed and produced by students of the Inner Temple, one of the law schools of London, in the Christmas season of 1561-62. It is considered the first regular English tragedy. Whatever glory the Inner Temple achieved with its production, it held unchallenged for five years. Then another Inn of Court, Gray's Inn, resolved to try for a share of the dramatic glory. George Gascoigne, a gifted writer who had left the Inn about a decade earlier, had just returned, a mature man, to complete his studies. During the year 1566 he composed not one, but two, plays for his fellow students, one a comedy, the other a tragedy. The comedy was *The Supposes,* an admirable free translation (to say adaptation would not be far wrong) of Ariosto's *I Suppositi.* To the student of the English drama the first obvious distinction of this play is the fact that it is written in prose. All English plays up to this time had been written in verse.

The play is far and away a better play than *Gorboduc*— almost inevitably so, since Ariosto's comedy was patterned after Roman comedy, which was far and away better theater than the Roman pseudo-Senecan tragedy, which served as a model for *Gorboduc.* It was a rule of classical tragedy that no violent action take place in the presence of the audience; all such action to be accomplished behind the scenes, and to be reported by eye-witnesses. This left nothing but talk for the visible play. Thus *Gorboduc* consists of a series of long-winded speeches, in blank verse which is intended to be dignified, but which is in reality stiff and monotonous. Gascoigne's *Supposes,* on the other hand, is written in very good prose, a prose that is remarkably light and elastic for so early a period. The dialogue is lively and witty. The stage business is entertaining. The outline of the story may be omitted, since it is nothing else than the familiar sub-plot of Shakespeare's *Taming of the Shrew.* Yet be it emphasized that if Shakespeare had not incorporated the play in one of his works, it would still command our interest on its own merits. Professor Gayley, carried away with enthusiasm, speaks of it in this wise:

1 should be inclined to say that it was the first English comedy in

every way worthy of the name. It certainly is, for many reasons, entitled to be called the first comedy in the English tongue. It is written, not for the children, nor to educate, but for grown-ups, and solely to delight. It is done into English, not for the vulgar, but for the more advanced taste of the translator's own Inn of Court. It has, therefore, qualities to captivate those who are capable of appreciating high comedy. It is composed, like its original, in straightforward, sparkling prose ... It combines character and situation, each depending upon the other. Without historical apology or artistic concessions it would act well today.

This is high praise, and in a general way I should subscribe to it. When Professor Gayley thus cavalierly brushes aside all predecessors of the *Supposes* in English comedy, he is not thinking of the comedy efforts to which we have already given attention, namely, the plays of Henry Medwall, John Rastell, John Heywood, and Sir Thomas More. They are too insubstantial, where they are not frankly farcical, to be real competitors of such a play as the *Supposes*. He has in mind, particularly, two plays which the textbooks commonly give as the first English comedies, namely, the two school plays, *Gammer Gurton's Needle* and *Ralph Roister Doister,* both antedating the *Supposes* by nearly fifteen years. Either of the two might, not without reason, challenge Gayley's verdict.

The tragedy with which Gascoigne provided his fellow-students during the same year (1566), he penned in collaboration with another student, named Francis Kinwelmershe. It is entitled *Jocasta,* and is described on the title-page as "A Tragedie written in Greeke by Euripides, translated and digested into Acte by George Gascoygne and Francis Kinwelmershe of Grayes Inne, and there by them presented, 1566."

I have quoted this title-page in full for the simple reason that it is a brazen falsehood. The authors wish to give the impression that they have translated Euripides' *Phoenician Women* out of the original Greek. The fact is that their work is a rendering of an Italian translation by Lodovico Dolce. Furthermore, Dolce himself knew no Greek, his version being a rendering of a Latin translation printed in 1541; so that the version by Gascoigne and Kinwelmershe is a translation of a translation of a translation. All of which is of no great importance to us just now. What *is* important is the nature of the tragedy thus presented to compete for glory with *Gorboduc,* the product of a rival institution.

We saw that *Gorboduc* was written in the Senecan style. We must now say a word more about the plot. It will be recalled that a father is called upon, but in vain, to attempt to prevent his two sons from waging war against each other to settle a dispute respecting conflicting claims to the throne. Those who are familiar with the story of the sons of Oedipus must at once be struck by the resemblance, the difference being that in the Greek legend it is the mother, not the father, who attempts to bring about reconciliation. The story was told by Aeschylus, Euripides, and Seneca. The two young law students, Sackville and Norton, probably got the idea from Seneca. But they did not want to be mere copy-cats. They wanted to be original. Making the father instead of the mother the central figure is one original touch. Having the conflict precipitated by the father's unwise division of his kingdom is another. But the most noteworthy departure from the model lies in the transfer of the scene of action from ancient Greece to ancient Britain. The authors would thus be justified in considering their play as their own creation. The dialogue certainly was.

Gascoigne and Kinwelmershe, on the other hand, laid no claim to originality. Gascoigne frankly stated on the title-page of his comedy, *Supposes,* that it was "A Comedie written in the Italian tongue by Ariosto, Englished by George Gascoygne of Grayes Inne, Esquire." And as to the tragedy, *Jocasta,* Gascoigne and Kinwelmershe admitted that it was a translation, though they fibbed regarding the original. What is significant is their deliberate use of the very same story from which the authors of *Gorboduc* got their idea. Furthermore, they followed the example of those authors in employing blank verse. *Jocasta* was thus the second play in the English language to employ the medium which the Elizabethans were soon to recognize as the one suitable medium for tragedy.

Scholars used to make comparisons between *Jocasta* and the original play by Euripides—much to the discredit of the former. But that was before it was discovered that Lodovico Dolce, not Euripides, had been translated by Gascoigne and Kinwelmershe. Much of the unfavorable criticism really applied to the Italian version. But not all of it. When Dolce showed bad taste Gascoigne was very apt to go him one better. Thus Oedipus' simple outcry, "O mother, O miserable wife!", is expanded by Dolce into five lines. But his rendering does not sound as ludicrous as Gascoigne's:

> O wife, O mother, O both woeful names!
> O woeful mother, and O woeful wife!
> O would to God, alas! O would to God,
> Thou ne'er had been my mother nor my wife!

This sounds absurd to us; but it must have pleased the untrained ear of the early Elizabethans, for such ejaculations became popular. Even Shakespeare succumbed to the vogue. Witness the following in the early *Romeo and Juliet:*

> *Nurse.* O woe! O woeful, woeful, woeful day!
> O day! O day! O day! O hateful day!
> O woeful day, O woeful day!
> *Paris.* O love! O life! not life, but love in death!
> *Capulet.* O child! O child! my soul and not my child!

Shakespeare's taste, however, improved rapidly, and in *A Midsummer Night's Dream* he burlesqued the fustian:

> O grim-look'd night! O night with hue so black!
> O night, which ever art when day is not!
> O night, O night, alack, alack, alack.
> I fear my Thisbe's promise is forgot!

Altogether *Jocasta* is a disappointing achievement after the excellent talent displayed in *Supposes*. Certainly it shows no advance on *Gorboduc.* The latter may be stiff and monotonous, but it is not ludicrous. The Inner Temple surely did not feel that it had surrendered its laurels to Gray's Inn. Gascoigne's comedy would not worry it, for comedy was a species that nobody respected anyhow. Even a score of years later Thomas Kyd could say:

> A comedy!
> Fie! comedies are fit for common wits:

But to present a kingly troupe withal,
Give me a stately-written tragedy;
 Tragoedia cothurnata, fitting kings,
Containing matter, and not common things.

And in *Gorboduc* the Inner Temple must have felt that it had produced "a stately-written tragedy" that Gray's Inn had not equalled.

Nevertheless, the Inner Temple was going to show Gray's Inn that it had not exhausted itself in its first effort. Accordingly, five of its students got together to write another tragedy. They probably had contempt for their rival's lack of originality. Both its comedy and its tragedy had been translations, and the style of its tragedy had been borrowed from *Gorboduc*. This time they were going to change both the style and the material. Instead of blank verse they would employ rhyme and instead of resorting to the legendary past for their story, they would do what Gray's Inn had done: go to Italy. They would not take a completed work and merely translate it; they would explore the new and rich field of the Italian *novelle* (later so profitably explored by Shakespeare) for a suitable story and write a romantic drama of love. Their story they got from Boccaccio, and the following year—that is, early in 1568—they were ready to produce before the Queen their tragedy of *Gismonde of Salerne*.

They slyly let their rivals know that they knew very well that it was Dolce, and not Euripides, that Gascoigne had translated, by supplying their play with a prologue which was patterned after the prologue to one of Dolce's plays, as if to say: "You see, we have read our Dolce; you cannot fool us."

The plot is a highly dramatic one. Gismonde, daughter of King Tancred, is carrying on a secret affair with Guiscard. When her father discovers the secret he has Guiscard killed, and sends the lover's bloody heart in a golden goblet to his daughter, who adds poison to the contents and drinks them down. The father is then smitten with remorse, and decides to commit suicide in the single tomb prepared for the two lovers.

Here is the first extant play to exploit the passion of love, a forerunner of *Romeo and Juliet*. Though the story is a romantic one, drawn from a modern Italian novel, yet the construction of the play, like that of *Gorboduc* and *Jocasta,* is on the strictly classical lines prescribed by the Latin plays attributed to the Roman philosopher, Seneca. In fact, the course of the action follows, almost scene by scene, one of the Senecan plays, the *Hippolytus.*

The rivalry between the two Inns was now suspended. However, twenty years later Gray's Inn was again stirred to dramatic activity, and came out in 1587-88 with a Senecan-type play, *The Misfortunes of Arthur,* the material drawn, as in *Gorboduc,* from legendary English history, and in the production of which Francis Bacon had a share. Possibly prompted by this production, Robert Wilmot, one of the five who had authored *Gismond of Salerne,* decided in 1591-92 to rewrite that play "according to the decorum of these daies"; that is, to bring it in line with the practice of such men as Thomas Kyd, Christopher Marlowe, Robert Greene and William Shakespeare. A comparison between the two versions is a lesson in the evolution of the English drama during the preceding quarter of a century. [1]   The example of a scholar prompted to literary activity apparently by a desire to enhance the honor of the Inner Temple and avowing his contempt for the public theater, as he did, falling nevertheless into the irresistible grip of that theater, is an eloquent lesson on the vitality of the dramatic forces of the period.

1; Cf. the present writer's article, "According to the Decorum of these Daies," *PMLA,* XXXIII (1918).

VIII. EARLY DAWN

The plays of Thomas Kyd, John Lyly and Christopher Marlowe that sprouted in the eighties of the sixteenth century do· not mark a progressive advance upon the drama preceding. They represent a giant leap toward greatness. There is no transition. A mere skeletal outline of one of the extant plays (there are not many) of the period will suffice to enable one to comprehend the magnitude of the task boldly undertaken by Marlowe to rescue the English drama "from jigging veins of rhyming mother wits, and such conceits as clownage keeps in pay." The play *Appius and Virginia* by Richard Bower will serve as an example. It was acted about 1563, thus giving us an idea of the state of the English drama at the time Shakespeare was born. It tells the story of the father Virginius who, at the earnest supplication of his daughter, Virginia, consents to take her life in order to save her honor from the attack of the lecherous Judge Appius.

The work possesses special interest in that it illustrates the transition from the medieval Morality described on page 1, to the modern secular play. The moral which the play sets out to teach is pronounced by the Prologue:

> Virgins you, O ladies fair, for honor of your name,
> Do lead the life apparent here to win immortal fame.
> Let not the blinded God of Love, as poets term him so,
> Nor Venus with her venery, nor lechers, cause of woe,
> Your virgins' name to spot or file. Dear dames, observe the life
> That fair Virginia did observe, who rather wished the knife
> Of father's hand her life to end, than spot her chastity.

Farther on he promises that if his audience patiently receive this, his first attempt, he would do better next time. Perhaps it is to the credit of his public that he was not, so far as we know, persuaded to try again.

The play proper opens with a soliloquy by Virginius, in which he expresses his pride in the superior chastity of his wife and his daughter. These presently enter, and there ensues a conversation between the three into which a premonitory note is injected. To this the daughter, Virginia, objects:

> O father, my comfort, O mother, my joy,
> O dear and O sovereign, do cease to employ
> Such dolorous talking, where dangers are none:
> Where joys are attendant, what needeth this moan?
> You matron, you spouse, you nurse and you wife,
> You comfort, you only the sum of his life:
> You husband, you sweetheart, you joy, and you pleasure,
> You king and you kaiser too, her only treasure;
> You father, you mother, my life doth sustain,
> I your babe, I your bliss, I your health am again.
> Forbear then your dolor, let mirth be frequented,
> Let sorrow depart, and not be attempted.

The atmosphere thus being cleared of all annoyance, all three sing in chorus:

> The trustiest treasure in earth, as we see,
> Is man, wife, and children, in one to agree;
> Then friendly and kindly, let measure be mixed
> With reason in season, where friendship is fixed.

These lines serve as a refrain for four solo stanzas, sung in rotation.

When they are through they depart, and the stage direction reads: *"Here entereth Haphazard the Vice."* The Vice was a stock figure in the Moralities. Out of his curious evolution in the history of the English theater emerged such diverse characters as the villain and the clown—even such creations as Falstaff and Autolicus. In the play under discussion he is both villain and clown. Upon his appearance he introduces himself:

> A proper gentleman I am, of truth:
> Yea, that may ye see by my long side-gown.
> Yea, but what am I? a scholar, or a schoolmaster, or else
>   some youth,
> A lawyer, a student, or else a country clown?

He follows this up with a long and rapid enumeration of his multifarious functions which reminds one, for all the world, of Figaro's report of the bewildering calls upon his services, in the opera.

Now it is time to set the comic interlude into full swing.

Servants enter and start the inescapable fisticuffs, in which, of course, the woman thrashes the man (the stage direction reads, *"Beat and hustle him"*). Haphazard makes an effort to intervene:

> What culling, what lulling, what stir have we here?
> What tugging, what lugging, what pugging by the ear?
> What, part and be friends, and end all this strife.

The brawl nevertheless continues a while longer. When, finally, reconciliation is achieved, the group get together to sing about their contempt for their masters:

> What if my lording do chance for to miss me,
> The worst that can happen is cudgel will kiss me:
> In such kind of sweetness, I swear by God's mother,
> It will please me better, it were on some other.
> With thwick thwack, with thump thump,
> With bobbing and bum,
> Our side-saddle shoulders shall shield that shall come.
> Hope so, and hap so, in hazard of threat'ning,
> The worst that can hap, lo, in end is but beating.

The last five lines serve as a refrain for four additional stanzas. Haphazard closes the scene with the couplet addressed to the audience:

> Well, fare ye well now for better or worse:
> Put hands to your pockets, have mind to your purse.

Later in the play he again warns the audience against pickpockets.

In a long soliloquy beginning, "The furrowed face of fortune's force my pinching pain doth move," Appius pours out his hopeless passion for the beautiful Virginia, winding up with, "O that my years were youthful yet, or that I were unwedded!" The bustling Haphazard appears opportunely, and suggests a simple plan whereby Appius, all-powerful ruler that he is, can get possession of the "fair Virginia." All he has to do is get someone to accuse Virginius of kidnapping the girl when she was an infant, and then to order him to bring her to court. After struggling with some scruples, which Haphazard dispels, he accepts the plan. Conscience and Justice enter and bewail their unhappy plight.

After some more tomfoolery on the part of the singing quartet led by Haphazard, Virginius is called to court, is accused, and is informed by Rumor what Appius' real intention is. This information he conveys to his daughter, who implores him to take her life:

> O father, O friendship, O fatherly favor,
> Whose dulcet words so sweetly do savor,
> On knees I beseech thee to grant my request,
> In all things according as liketh thee best.
> Thou knowest, O my father, if I be once spotted,
> My name and my kindred then forth will be blotted.
> Then rather, dear father, if it be thy pleasure,
> Grant me the death, then keep I my treasure,
> My lamp, my light, my life undefiled.
> This upon my knees with humble behest,
> Grant me, my father, my instant request.
> *Virginius.* O daughter, O dear, O darling, O dame,
> Dispatch *me,* I pray thee, regard not my name.
> But yet as thou sayest, with remedy none,
> And better it is to die with good fame,
> Than longer to live to reap us but shame.
> But if thou do die no doubt is at all,
> But presently after myself follow shall,
> Then end without shame, so let us persever,
> With trump of good fame, so die shall we never.

The stage direction reads: *"Here tie a handkercher about her eyes, and then strike off her head."* Having accomplished the deed (how, it is difficult to imagine) he is prevented from slaying himself by Comfort, who advises him to carry the head to Appius.

Appius condemns Virginius to death, and calls upon Justice and Reward to carry out the sentence. They both enter, and Justice addresses Appius:

> O gorgon judge, what lawless life hast thou most wicked led!
> Thy soaking sin hath sunk thy soul, thy virtues all are fled.
> Thou chaste and undefiled life did seek for to have spotted,
> And thy reward is ready here, by Justice now allotted.

> *Reward.* Thy just reward is deadly death; wherefore
> come, wend away:
> To death I straight will do thy corpse; then lust shall
> have his prey.
> Virginius, thou woeful knight, come near and take thy foe.
> In prison do thou make him fast: no more let him do so.

At this point Haphazard rushes in, and, unaware of the situation, calls upon Appius for his reward. Receiving no attention from Appius, he turns directly to Reward and Justice:

> All hail, Master Reward, and righteous Justice:
> I beseech you let me be recompensed too, according
> to my service;
> For why all this long time I have lived in hope.
> *Reward.* Then for thy reward, then, here is a rope.

Haphazard doesn't at all like the idea of hanging. He looks ruefully at the rope and murmurs:

> Must I needs hang? by the gods, it doth spite me
> To think how crabbedly this silk lace will bite me.

Fame, Doctrina, and Memory come in bearing a tomb, on which Memory writes:

> I, Memory, will mind her life: her death shall ever reign
> Within the mouth and mind of man, from age to age again.

And the play closes with the Epilogue emphasizing the moral and repeating a prayer for the Queen.

The speeches quoted have been severely abridged, but they suffice to illustrate what Marlowe had in mind when he spoke of the "jigging veins of rhyming mother wits," and the diction that Shakespeare burlesqued in *The Most Lamentable Comedy, and Most Cruel Death of Pyramus and Thisbe.*

In his preface to *Cambyses,* another play of the same period (Falstaff, in *Henry the Fourth,* announces that he would play the King in "King Cambyses' vein"), Hawkins makes the significant remark: "With the admirable comedy of *Ralph Roister Doister* (and he might have added *Gammer Gurton's Needle*) before their eyes, it might seem strange that later writers should have relapsed into comparative barbarism, if we had not abundant evidence of such degeneracy in every period of the history of our dramatic literature, including that which followed the publication of the unrivalled works of Shakespeare himself." Perhaps the remarkable thing is rather that those two isolated plays are as good as they are. A fair question would be why the authors seemed to have exhausted themselves each with a single play of such promise. Evidently the spirit of the age was not such as to stimulate literary creation. An inkling of what that spirit was may be derived from the fact that the author of *Ralph Roister Doister,* Nicholas Udall, was once arrested for having a copy of Tyndale's translation of the New Testament in his possession. In all likelihood both these authors would have done more, and better, a third of a century later, when English life was effervescent with excitement over newly discovered mental and physical realms.

Incidentally, Hawkins takes it for granted that *Ralph Roister Doister* and, presumably, *Gammer Gurton's Needle,* were "before their eyes." In all probability they were not. They were not printed until later. Possibly their availability would have had a favorable influence.

IX.   THE "LITTLE EYASES"

Hamlet. What players are they?

Rosencrantz. Even those you were wont to take such delight in, the tragedians of the city.

Hamlet. How chances they travel? ... Do they hold the same estimation they did when I was in the city? Are they followed?

Rosencrantz. No, indeed, they are not.

Hamlet. How comes it? Do they grow rusty?

Rosencrantz. Nay, their endeavor keeps in the wonted pace; but there is, sir, an eyrie of children, little eyases, that cry out on top of question and are most tyrannically clapped for't; these are now the fashion.

Hamlet. What, **are they children?**

If Shakespeare felt impelled to embark upon the foregoing digression, it behooves us to look into the history of these "little eyases," these boy actors whose competition the adult companies could not meet. The beginning of that story goes back almost a century. The coming of the Renaissance impelled people to seek ways and means to satisfy their new-born appetite for pleasure. At the court of England this quest for pleasure resulted in the development of what Milton later referred to as "mask and antique pageantry." A pageant was a gorgeous representation of pantomime and song, staged on a huge float fitted up to represent something big, like a mountain, or a castle. By the use of machinery the float could be made to undergo startling transformations. The occasion was a grand affair, in which everybody took part, from the king down to the professional entertainers. Henry VIII, a pleasure-loving monarch, spent money with lavish abandon on his pageants. On one of them, lasting two days, in 1511, he spent what was the equivalent of more than a million dollars today. The decorations and costumes were of the finest materials the world had to offer. The buttons, for example, were of real gold. At the end of the performance there was a riot, in which the courtly audience made a dash for "souvenirs." Even the buttons on the king's coat were ripped off. The float, or stage, of course was wrecked. At subsequent affairs, to obviate the repetition of such a scandalous scene, the king made a present of the costumes to the actors that wore them. These, we may be sure, made themselves scarce before the storm could break. Lucky actors!—particularly those that played more than one part. Nothing, however, could save the stage—that was always wrecked.

The mask, which Milton couples with pageantry, was a device borrowed from Italy—a sort of dramatic entertainment in which a slight plot on a fantastic theme served as an excuse for dialogue, singing, dancing, impersonation, and spectacular display. It therefore resembled the modern musical comedy. A fine example of the mask is Milton's *Comus,* in which the slight plot serves also as an excuse for some beautiful poetry.

The pageant and the mask maintained a degree of popularity at the English court for a long time. To be sure, Elizabeth, who was a parsimonious queen, restricted her indulgence in them, and encouraged the less expensive production of regular plays—a fortunate thing for the English drama. At the court of her Stuart successors, however, the mask, having absorbed the characteristics of the pageant, attained a high state of artistic excellence, particularly at the hands of Shakespeare's younger contemporary, Ben Jonson.

It now remains to find the link that connected the mask with the Elizabethan drama. That link, sensational as it may seem, was forged by acting companies made up entirely of boys. This is how it came about.

Among those who took part in the masks staged by Henry VIII was the royal choir, known as the Chapel Royal. The man selected to lead this choir was always the best musician in the land; but Henry VIII was fortunate in having as leader a man who was a versatile genius. Not only was he a singer and composer; he also had a gift for poetry and, as it turned out, for playwriting and stage management. This man's name was William Cornish. He was on the alert to meet the king's demand for novelty and variety. His choir consisted of twenty-four men and eight boys. It was primarily, of course, a musical organization. But is there anything extraordinary about combining music with acting? The ancient Greek theater and the modern opera house show that it is quite natural. In 1512 Cornish introduced the mask from Italy. With time the musical element of the entertainment was made less prominent and the acting element more so. The distinguished poet John Masefield has observed that nearly all children make good actors, while few adults do. It must therefore have been found increasingly difficult to get men who could both sing and act, so that men were used less and less, and after 1553, the year in which Mary became queen, they were never again called upon to act.

Cornish died in 1523, and the musicians that succeeded him in office had no talent for the drama. But dramatic performances by the choir were now an established tradition, so the king engaged John Heywood to take charge of its theatrical activities. On the accession of Mary, in 1553, Heywood's place was taken by a talented schoolmaster, Nicholas Udall. As a scholar, he naturally thought that the best way to write plays was in the manner of the Romans, and in that manner is written his best known play, *Ralph Roister Doister.*

In 1561, Richard Edwards took charge of the Chapel Royal. In his day he was extravagantly praised as a playwright. To us the extant example of his work, *Damon and Pythias*, is crude and amateurish, but it marks the stage arrived at in the evolution of the English drama at the time Shakespeare was born. At last plays were being written that could compare favorably with the plays produced more than a third of a century earlier by the group of writers associated with Cardinal Morton's household. During the two dozen years which elapsed before Shakespeare came to London, the English drama was destined to undergo some interesting developments under new and interesting conditions.

In 1564 (the very year in which Shakespeare was born), one of the Chapel Royal choir boys, named Richard Farrant, having grown to manhood, was appointed Master of the choir boys at Windsor. What could be more natural than that he, a graduate from a choir that had honorable dramatic traditions, should promptly set to work to train his boys as actors? He did this so well that until his death his troupe acted almost every Christmas before the Queen. He must have possessed unusual enterprise, for when, in 1576, James Burbage built his theater (the only regular theater in England) in the suburbs of London, he conceived an extraordinary idea, and proceeded to carry it through. That idea was to get a theater of his own, more conveniently located, and use the boys as his actors. A man of less enterprise and ingenuity would have seen two insurmountable difficulties: first, that the boys belonged to the Queen, as her choir boys, and could not be turned into professional actors in a public theater; second, that the London authorities were opposed to the erection of public playhouses. Farrant resolved both difficulties into one, and proceeded to solve it. His performances were not to be public performances in a public theater, but private rehearsals in a private theater, to which the public was invited. That he would charge admission to the rehearsals was only incidental. He claimed that his boys needed practice before an audience in order to make a creditable showing before the Queen. Thus prepared to disarm opposition he, with brazen audacity, leased a suitable apartment in the Blackfriars district, one of the most fashionable in London, made the necessary alterations, and built the first indoor theater in England, known as the First Blackfriars Theater.

The residents of the neighborhood naturally objected; but Farrant held his own until he died, four years later, when William Hunnis, Master of the Children of the Chapel Royal, secured the lease from Farrant's widow. But the owner of the building in which the theater was housed vexed him with lawsuits in an attempt to recover possession. A series of subleasings with the purpose of obstructing the efforts of the landlord, resulted, in 1583, in the lease falling into the hands of the Earl of Oxford, a patron of the drama, who promptly presented it to his favorite, John Lyly.

Lyly was a man of college education and high literary ability, and this was his great opportunity. Incidentally, it was the great opportunity of the English drama too. At last plays were to be written for the English public by a man who was not only a practical playwright, but one whose artistic sense had been trained, and who, therefore, could give the English drama artistic form.

Lyly's plans were ambitious ones. For the plays he had in mind he needed more actors than the twelve boys that now made up the Chapel Royal. So he entered into an agreement with the Master of the Children of St. Paul's, whereby he could use those boys also. For this combined troupe he wrote (or, possibly, revised from earlier versions of his) in quick succession, the two comedies, *Alexander and Campaspe* and *Sappho and Phao,* characterized by sparkling wit and clever repartee. Moreover, he also induced another gifted young college man, George Peele, who had been active in dramatics at Oxford, to join him in the enterprise, and Peele at once wrote, in the style set by Lyly, *The Arraignment of Paris.* The Roman five-act division which Udall had employed, Lyly and Peele also adopted, and apparently the English plays felt quite at home with it, for it became the accepted form for English drama down almost to our own generation. These three plays were thus the first modern five-act plays produced before the general public in an English theater.

Lyly's occupancy of Farrant's playhouse lasted only one year. In 1584 the landlord succeeded in recovering possession, and that meant the end of the First Blackfriars Theater. But it had accomplished its task. Neither Lyly nor Peele could now be stopped. Lyly continued to write for the Paul's boys, using some building connected with the cathedral (possibly the singing school) as a theater. Here Shakespeare saw them act when he arrived in London a few years later, and let the plays which Lyly wrote for them serve as models for the comedies with which he launched his career as a dramatist. Thus it is no exaggeration to say that the development of the English drama, to the point where Shakespeare took it up, was accomplished through the medium of troupes of boys.

Children's companies continued to act until the theaters were closed by the Puritans in 1642. Their importance in relation to the adult companies may be measured by the concern expressed in the dialogue with which this chapter opens. Shakespeare never wrote for them; but those that did were among his greatest contemporaries.

X. THE ACTING PROFESSION IN SHAKESPEARE'S TIME

In the sixteenth century the demand for theatrical entertainment was widespread. This demand resulted in the organization of numerous troupes of performers that traveled back and forth across the country, and the rapid increase in their number as the century advanced is a measure of the increase in the demand. It is impossible to estimate the number of groups of irresponsible vagabonds that offered wayside entertainment of one sort or another; but of legally constituted companies there have been counted more than fifty for the half century preceding the accession of Elizabeth, while for her entire reign uncompleted researches have revealed more than one hundred and fifty. A legally constituted company was one that fitted itself into the feudal organization of the country by registering as the servants of some noble, who was then known as its patron. Sometimes the patron would take an active interest in the welfare of his company. He might be a patron of the drama, or possibly a writer of plays himself, and so would need his troupe to exploit his works. The patron's interest might be encouraged by the scheming of a thoughtful wife, as was the case of Lady Derby, who sought to keep her husband interested in the players "for my lord taking delight in them it will keep him from more prodigal courses." Usually, however, the relation between troupe and patron was hardly more than a formality. He would merely supply them with credentials that would protect them in their travels against arrest as vagabonds.

A strolling troupe, in the earlier part of the century, usually consisted of four men and a boy–the boy to act female parts; for it was inconceivable, in the England of those days, for a woman to act. As late as 1629, the actresses in a French troupe visiting London were hooted from the boards. Later the number of members increased, particularly in companies that established themselves in London. Shakespeare's company in 1592 contained at least twenty-three, and in 1624 about forty, counting all hands.

The members of a strolling company had to be versatile. Not only did they have to be actors, they had to be musicians and acrobats. These qualifications give us an inkling of the kind of entertainment they afforded, and the kind of plays they produced. What is said of the versatility of the strolling players applies in large measure to the important companies established in London. For instance, three of the very best actors in Shakespeare's organization at one time toured Europe with a troupe of acrobats.

Naturally the best actors gravitated to London, where they played in inn-yards; and Shakespeare's company usually had three or four adult rivals regularly established in the metropolis. But adverse local conditions, like municipal opposition, competition, or more particularly, the plague, would often drive them back into the provinces. Sometimes a talented actor, illustrating the proverb, would join a troupe of strolling players in order to be first in the village rather than second in Rome. Dekker speaks of some "who, out of an ambition to wear the best jerkin in a strolling company, or to act great parts, forsake the stately and our more than Roman city stages, to travel upon the hard hoof from village to village for cheese and buttermilk." One such individual got a rebuke from the notorious highwayman, Gamaliel Ratsey: "And for you, sirrah, thou hast a good presence upon a stage; methinks thou darkenst thy merit by playing in the country. Get thee to London, for, if one man were dead [probably referring to Burbage] they will have much need of such a one as thou art." Occasionally, instead of traveling through England, a company would make a tour of the continent, particularly the Germanic territory, where they were very popular, and where they exerted a potent influence on the development of the drama. "We can be bankrupt on this side," players are represented as saying, "and gentlemen of a company beyond the sea: we burst at London, and are pieced up at Rotterdam." Sometimes a "pieced up" English troupe would remain permanently established "beyond the sea."

Numerous references in the plays and other contemporary references to the actor's art prove that the standard of excellence set for the actor was a high one, and further prove that the standard was attained. The German traveler, Thomas Platter, who witnessed a performance of *Julius Caesar* at the Globe, tells us that it was "acted extremely well." The widely traveled Fynes Moryson avers that "as there be, in my opinion, more plays in London than in all parts of the world I have seen, so do these players or comedians excel all others in the world."

He reports an instance: "I remember that when some of our cast despised stage players came out of England into Germany, and played at Frankford in the time of the mart, having neither a complete number of actors, nor any good apparel, nor any ornament of the stage, yet the Germans, not understanding a word they said, both men and women, flocked wonderfully to see their gesture and action." Concerning the leading actor in each of the two principal London companies, the Chamberlain's and the Admiral's, Sir Richard Baker, an acknowledged judge in such matters, declared that "Richard Burbage and Edward Alleyn were two such actors as no age must look to see again." In what high estimation the English actors were held on the continent, is illustrated in an anecdote reported by Thomas Nash. It concerns Willam Kemp, the comedian in Shakespeare's early plays: "Coming from Venice this last summer, and taking Bergamo in my way homeward to England, it was my hap, sojourning there some four or five days, to light in fellowship with that famous Francatrip harlequin, who, perceiving me to be an Englishman by my habit of speech, asked me many particulars of the order and manner of plays, which he termed by the name of representations. Amongst other talk, he inquired of me if I knew any such *Parabolano,* here in London, as *Signior Charlatino Kempino?* Very well, quoth I, and have been often in his company. He hearing me say so, began to embrace me anew, and offered me all the courtesy he could for his sake, saying, although he knew him not, yet for the report he had heard of his pleasance, he could not but be in love with his perfections, being absent." To insure good work on the part of the actors, the companies adopted rules severely penalizing absence from rehearsal.

Fynes Moryson's reference to "our cast despised stage players" reminds us of the social status of the actor in those days. The actors felt keenly the humiliation attending their occupation. Shakespeare expressed his feeling in the sonnets. Some players, including Shakespeare, attempted to buy respectability by securing a coat of arms. Yet it seems to be in keeping with human nature for us to pet and patronize what we consider beneath us; and the Elizabethan actor was thus petted and patronized. Dekker says it is the ambition of dandies who would be thought men of fashion to give banquets to actors, and

John Earle tells us that actors were the chief guests of the gentlemen of the Inns of Court, and the favorites of fine ladies. Ben Jonson, too, says of courtiers that "their glory is to invite players to suppers." We speak of "matinee idols" today. The Elizabethan actor was literally a matinee idol: he performed only in the afternoon.

The typical Elizabethan troupe contained a central group that constituted a stock company, in which the compensation of the actor was determined, not by the part he played, but by the number of shares he owned. This group hired other actors as they were needed, maintained apprentices for female parts, and bought plays, or entered into contract with playwrights. Sometimes individual members would own shares in a play-house also; but in no case did a company as a whole own its theater. Instead, it rented one, paying the owner half the income from the galleries as rent. Shakespeare's company, known as the Lord Chamberlain's men, was distinguished by the extraordinary spirit of comradeship that bound it together. The spirit was fostered by several peculiar features in its organization. One was the unusually large representation of its member-ship in the ownership of the two theaters in which it played, namely, the Globe and the Blackfriars; six of its principal members owning three-quarters of the shares in the former and six-sevenths of the shares in the latter. The only outsider, Cuthbert Burbage, was the brother of the leading actor, Richard Burbage, the greatest actor of his time. Furthermore, the shares were held in joint tenancy; which means that no share could be sold to an outsider. Another distinguishing feature was the fact that its chief playwright was also a principal member, and incidentally the greatest playwright of all time. All circum-stances were thus conducive to the fullest co-operation, with assurance of success. With the best organization, the greatest actor, and the greatest playwright, Shakespeare's company won first place among the London companies. When James I came to the throne and decided that all acting troupes must come under the direct patronage of the royal family instead of that of the nobility, there was nothing surprising in the fact that he took Shakespeare's company under his own personal patronage, when it ceased to be called the Lord Chamberlain's Men, and was thereafter known as His Majesty's Servants.

XI. SHAKESPEARE'S PLAYHOUSE

The earliest record of a building in England erected for the presentation of plays dates from 1524. It was built by John Rastell, brother-in-law of Thomas More, on his estate in the suburbs north of London. This information is derived from the extant record of a lawsuit over the loan of certain theatrical costumes. But that is all we know about it. We do not know when it ceased to be. At any rate, when Shakespeare was born there was no building in England devoted exclusively to theatrical purposes. Troupes of actors would set up a temporary stage in any available place, such as the public square, the town hall, or the inn-yard. In London the favorite place was the inn-yard. A moment's reflection will tell why. The galleries on which the rooms opened afforded very desirable viewpoints for the guests of the inn, and the yard itself could accommodate the crowd of outsiders. It was a simple matter for the actors to erect a temporary platform on some barrels against the side where the stables were situated, using for dressing rooms as much of the stabling as they needed.

The extraordinary expansion of national spirit which marked the accession of Elizabeth to the throne expressed itself, among other ways, in the increasing popularity of the drama. Acting companies multiplied and the demand for inn-yards increased, so much so that some enterprising innkeepers found it profitable to erect and equip permanent stages in their yards, thus making a strong bid for the patronage of the players. To all intents and purposes, these yards were converted into theaters, and were spoken of as such. In this way the more important companies were enabled to lease a particular "theater" and establish themselves permanently in London, traveling in the provinces (as they would say) or going on the road (as we should say) only when forced to do so by an outbreak of the plague in the city, or by some other adverse conditions. There were at least five of these "inns, or osteryes (hostelries) turned to playhouses."

But the path of the theatrical profession in London was not strewn with roses. The theater met with hostility from various quarters: from the city authorities, because the congregation of all sorts and conditions of men and women was not calculated to simplify the task of maintaining order in the city; from the merchants and tradespeople, because the playhouse lured the apprentices from their work, and also because they naturally objected to the inroads which the play-going habit made upon the purses of the citizens; above all, from the Puritans and the clergy. To the Puritans, playhouses were "seminaries of impiety, no better than houses of bawdry." The clergy, besides being outraged by the fact that plays were given on Sundays, and that the female parts were played by males in the face of the biblical prohibition for males to dress as females, felt aggrieved that ·their efforts could not compete with those of the actors. The Reverend John Stockwood bitterly complains: "Will not a filthy play, with the blast of a trumpet sooner call together a thousand than an hour's tolling of the bell bring to the sermon a hundred?—nay, even here in the city, where shall you find a reasonable company?—whereas, if you resort to The Theater, The Curtain, and other places of plays in the city, you shall on the Lord's Day have these places so full as possibly they can throng."

In the face of such strong and determined opposition the players could not have survived but for the unfailing encouragement and support of the court. The Queen herself took a personal interest in their welfare, in one instance issuing strict orders to the city authorities, "willing and commanding you, as ye tender our pleasure, to permit and suffer them herein without any of your lets, hindrances, or molestations." Nevertheless, the city authorities found, within their rights, ways and means of practicing their "lets, hindrances, and molestations"; · and although in their diplomatic contests with the court their triumphs were never of long duration, these harassed the actors, and were among the adverse local conditions alluded to above, which sent them into the provinces.

One more obstacle we must not fail to mention, one that was of a different kind from those already enumerated, yet one that had decidedly practical bearings, namely, the fact that performances could not be given every day in the inn-yards, as these were also used as freight stations by the carriers, or, as we should say, the express companies. In fact, some of the yards were available for theatrical purposes only once a week, and none of them were so available more than three times a week.

This made it hard for the actors to make a living.

Finally, in 1576, two men put their heads together. One was John Brayne (a significant name) who was the owner of one of the inns, and who therefore knew from experience how profitable was the renting of quarters to theatrical troupes. The other was his brother-in-law, James Burbage, an actor and manager of a company of players, who knew therefore what a substantial portion of the box office receipts had to be handed over as rent to the inn-keeper. The upshot was that these two men decided to build a theater of their own. And they would build it where the city fathers could not lay their hands on it—which meant outside the city limits.

They found a suitable location in Shoreditch, only half a mile to the north, and received a twenty-one-year lease on a piece of property there. They were doubly protected from interference, in that the place was within the grounds of the dissolved priory of Holy Well, therefore under the direct jurisdiction of the Crown. The enterprising borthers-in-law must have had visions of gold, for in order tc finance the undertaking Burbage borrowed right and left and Brayne sold the grocery business he was running and the lease on his house, and even went so far as to pawn his clothes. Thus the first theater in England of which we have any substantial knowledge came to be built; and the owners had practical advertising sense enough to name it "The Theater."

How were they to design their playhouse? Since there can be nothing absolutely new under the sun, they had to model it on the only playhouse they had ever seen—the old inn-yard, with the inn omitted. But whereas the inn-yard was rectangular, they made their theater octagonal, because they were practical enough to take a hint from the round bear ring, in which great crowds assembled to witness bear-baiting. In the construction of later playhouses, practical experience must have suggested changes and improvements in minor details; but, in a general way they all resembled the first playhouse. One of these, the Fortune, built in 1599, returned to the rectangular shape of the inn-yard; but that the owners saw the unwisdom of this proceeding is proved by the fact that when the Fortune burned down in 1621, the building that replaced it was built round.

The Theater became one of the sights of London. It was

spoken of as "gorgeous," as "sumptuous." An unintended compliment comes from a Puritan: "It is an evident token of a wicked time when players wax so rich that they can build such houses." The idea evidently was considered a good one, for within a few months two more playhouses were erected. The Curtain (named after the Curtain estate on which it was built) was put up, nobody knows how or by whom, in the same neighborhood, only a few hundred yards to the south. The other, known as the First Blackfriars Theater, built by Richard Farrant, was not an open-air theater, and so deserves particularly to be remembered as the first regular indoor theater in England. Its story is told in another chapter.

When James Burbage secured from Gyles Alleyn the lease on the property on part of which he was to erect his playhouse, it was agreed that the lease was to run for twenty-one years; but that if Burbage, before the expiration of ten years, spent two hundred pounds renovating the dilapidated tenements on the property, he would, when the ten years were up, be entitled to a new lease to run for twenty-one years from that date; and furthermore, that he would have the right, before the original twenty-one years expired, to tear down and remove any buildings he might have erected. Burbage fulfilled the required conditions, but when the end of the ten years was approaching, and Burbage applied for a new lease, Alleyn evaded the question, and managed, in one way or another, to hold Burbage off from year to year.

Burbage was no fool, and he saw trouble ahead. A calamity threatened. He might lose his playhouse! He decided, therefore, to act betimes and be ready for an emergency. He would build another theater. This time he was going to follow Farrant's example and build an indoor theater. Accordingly, he purchased a building in the Blackfriars district, adjoining the house in which Farrant had built his playhouse. Removing the partitions on the second floor, which had a very high ceiling, gave him a large room, sixty-six feet long and forty-six feet wide, which he provided with two balconies, and otherwise equipped it as a playhouse.

But here he struck a snag. The Blackfriars district was a highly aristocratic residential section. When the report got around that a common playhouse was to be opened in the neighborhood, consternation prevailed. The residents quickly got together and sent a petition to the Privy Council begging it to forbid the opening of a new house. It was customary when a company of players was in trouble, for it to resort to its patron, a person of influence, to intercede in its behalf; and this intercession was usually successful. But what hope had Burbage now, when the very second name on the list of petitioners was none other than that of his own patron, Lord Hunsdon? The shock was too much for him, and he died soon after.

Only two months remained before the expiration of the lease on The Theater. Burbage's two sons, Cuthbert and Richard, took the matter up with Alleyn, but the scheming landlord merely offered vague encouragement, until the term had finally expired, and the Burbages no longer had the right to remove the playhouse. But the two brothers had inherited their father's enterprise, and were determined not to be outwitted.

They quickly acquired a suitable piece of ground on the south side of the Thames, which by this time had become a theatrical center. Then, while Alleyn was away in the country, they engaged a crew of workmen, who, in the stillness of the night, set about to tear down the memorable structure their father had erected. Before Alleyn was able to get wind of what had happened, the timbers were safely deposited on the newly acquired plot, and were presently used to erect there a new playhouse, which was named the Globe, and which was destined to be the scene of Shakespeare's greatest glory, and, next to the Theater of Dionysos in ancient Athens, the most memorable theater the world has ever seen. It was opened in the spring of 1599.

But we are not by any means through with the Blackfriars Theater. Before long the Burbage brothers succeeded in leasing it out as a "private" theater for a troupe of choir boys. In 1608, however, they took possession of the house for their own company (opposition having apparently subsided) which acted there during the winter months, reserving the open-air Globe for the warmer months of the year.

It has been estimated that the larger Elizabethan theaters could accommodate two thousand or more. As to beauty, it is hard to say how much claim they could lay to that. The Londoner considered them beautiful, but we doubt the Londoner's taste. Certainly, there was no lack of desire to make them beautiful. For instance, the specifications for the Fortune Theater, carefully require that "all the principal and main posts of the said frame and stage forward shall be square and wrought pilaster-wise with the carved proportions called satyrs, to be placed and set on the top of every of the said posts." Compared with contemporary playhouses in other countries, they probably were quite pretentious. Coryat, an extensive traveler of the time, says that the theaters in Venice were "beggarly and bare in comparison of our stately playhouses in England." Nevertheless, Fynes Moryson, another traveler of the day, who had been profoundly impressed by the exquisite beauty of the Olympic Theater in Vicenza, was probably not far from the truth when he wrote: "The theaters at London in England for stage plays are more remarkable for the number and for the capacity, than for the building."

Why, of all the theaters in the London of that wonderful age, have we selected for special emphasis The Theater, the Second Blackfriars, and the Globe—all the product of the Burbage family's enterprise? Because they were erected for the company of actors to which Shakespeare belonged, and for which, exclusively, he wrote his immortal plays. In the London of today, there is nothing about the sites formerly occupied by these structures to suggest the glory that once was theirs. The spot where The Theater stood is now the northeast corner of Curtain Road and New Inn Yard. The neighborhood has the uninviting and untidy appearance characteristic of the environs of a freight station. Where the Globe stood, now stands Barclay's Brewery, on the south side of Park Street. The approximate location is marked by a tablet erected by the London City Council. The pilgrim who has the courage to seek out the Globe will be assisted by the map on page x. The site of the Blackfriars is more conveniently located, for it is occupied by the home of the London Times.

XII. THE STAGING OF A SHAKESPEAREAN PLAY

The typical stage in an Elizabethan open-air theater consisted of a platform that extended well out into the auditorium, on a level with the lowest of the three galleries—four or five feet above the floor. At the rear was an alcove that could be curtained off. This is known as the inner stage. Above this inner stage, in line with the second gallery, was a similar alcove, and also in line with the third gallery. Adjoining each side of these alcoves was a catercornered wall, containing a door at the first level, a balcony at the second. Projecting from the roof level was a marquee, supported at the forward end on two tall columns that appeared to rest on the stage, but surely went through it to the floor underneath. Under this the actors found protection in case of rain. The occupants of the galleries were of course protected to a degree; but the standees around the stage, the "groundlings," simply accepted the rain. That is how much the play meant to them. An onslaught of sleet and snow will not drive an American crowd from a football game. Superimposed on the marquee was a "hut" that rose above the roof. From it extended a flagpole, and in it was kept a large bell and machinery for thunder and other noises, as well as a device for lowering supernatural beings through a trap door in its floor. There were trap doors also on the floor of the stage, both inner and outer. These could serve, among other purposes, as graves into which the dead might be deposited, or from which ghosts might arise.

The staging of an Elizabethan production was of course conditioned by the construction of the stage just described. Most of the action took place on the main stage. Since this was never hidden from the audience, a scene on it could not open with the actors discovered in some dramatic situation. Their entrances had to be made part of the action; likewise their exits. All the characters had to leave the stage and the dead had to be carried out. That is why, in *Julius Caesar,* Caesar's body is carried out by Antony and the servant of Octavius, and later by the mob, who declare their intention to burn it in the holy place. Similarly, at the end of the play the body of Brutus is removed to Octavius' tent. The same difficulty was overcome in the same way even after the Restoration. In Villiers' *Rehearsal,* a play in which John Dryden is satirized under the name of Bayes, we read: "But, Mr. Bayes, how shall all these dead men go off? for I see none alive to help them." In a skirmish a character could resort to the simple device of falling off stage through a doorway or between the hangings hiding the inner stage.

For the same reason no thoroughgoing attempt could be made at realistic setting, only such properties being used as were needed to suggest the locality. They were brought on and carried off in full view of the audience. This, of course, as every theater-goer knows, is often done today too; only now there is a pretense of darkening the stage, and we good-naturedly make believe that we do not see the stage hands. If any heavy property, that could not be conveniently moved, was needed, it would be placed in the inner stage, which, as seen before, could be revealed or concealed by means of a curtain. In this way, for example, the stage could be set for the Senate House in the third act of *Julius Caesar.*

An action which was supposed to take place on an elevation, as in a balcony, on a wall, or on a hilltop, would be presented on the "upper stage," that is, the gallery at the back of the stage. There, for example, in *Julius Caesar,* Brutus and Mark Antony would stand to deliver their orations, and Pindarus would observe the movements of Titinius on the battlefield.

It seems clear that sometimes a removable stairway was used to connect the platform with the upper stage. It was not needed, however, to enable actors to get from one to the other (that function was adequately served by permanent stairs that belonged to the building and were probably situated behind the scenes); it would be employed only when the ascent or descent was itself part of the dramatic action.

A visit to the Dramatic Museum of Columbia University would well repay the student. There he would see models of the various types of stages and stage-settings that the western world has seen down to our own day. He would see that the tendency has been in the direction of absolute realism. Mr. Belasco's setting for *The Return of Peter Grimm* marks the ultimate development in this direction. It is a solidly built interior that is sure to provoke admiration. But the student must be cautioned against giving it unqualified preference in comparison with the

Elizabethan theater. It is easy to see that such an ideal of stage-setting confines the playwright within narrow limits. He cannot write a play requiring a change of scene, for example. The producer, too, can resort to a setting of this kind only when he believes that the play will have a long run. With it such a thing as a repertory theater, like Shakespeare's, is out of the question. Furthermore, it must be distinctly pointed out that the most recent developments in stage-craft have been emphatically away from the realistic setting, and in the direction of the manner of the Elizabethan theater.

This return to the older conception of staging is the result of a return to the older conception of the nature of the dramatic art. What this means is made clear by a presentation of one important difference between a Shakespearean production and a modern one. In a modern conservative theater, the audience is completely separated from the actors. The spectator is in front of a picture frame, inside of which he sees a painting with the figures animated. Even the foot-lights create a wall which emphasizes the inaccessibility of the world beyond. Now let us study the condition that obtained in Shakespeare's theater. There we find that the stage projected far out into the auditorium, with the result that the actors were completely surrounded by the spectators. Completely surrounded is correct; for not only did spectators occupy stools on the stage, but they also occupied the galleries above the stage, part of which was divided off into boxes known as the "Lords' Rooms," latticed in front to conceal the occupants from view. Thus there was intimacy between actors and audience. We compared the more modern production to painting. Correspondingly, we can compare the Shakespearean production to sculpture. It had three dimensions instead of two. In other words, according to the older conception, drama is plastic; according to the later one, it is pictorial. Which conception is better? "By their fruits ye shall know them." The plastic conception produced the Greek drama and the Elizabethan drama; and never since the death of Shakespeare has the theater held out so much promise as it does today, since we began to repudiate the realistic, pictorial stage.

However, while the Elizabethan stage manager disregarded realism in his setting, it was the object of his greatest care in other aspects of the production. The Elizabethan was hungry for realism, and demanded it even in minute details. If an eye was gouged out, or a heart torn out, there had to be a real eye, or a real heart, and real blood, and the local butcher was called upon to supply them. If a letter was supposed to be written in blood, red ink had to be used. The proximity of actor and spectator explains the necessity. If characters were supposed to have escaped from the sea, they had to come in dripping wet. The boys who played feminine roles were realistically made up, even being equipped with flesh-colored breasts. The same demand for realism explains the presence of so many anachronisms. Even if the scene was laid in antiquity, the characters, to the Elizabethan spectator, were not shades from a remote past, but beings like himself—of flesh and blood. They had to live as he lived, and dress as he dressed. Brutus' costume, then, would be like that of Sir Walter Raleigh, and Calpurnia's like that of Queen Elizabeth. And the costumes had to be genuine. There were no footlights to make shoddy material look like rich cloth. A company would pay only about six pounds for a play, but it did not hesitate to spend nineteen pounds for a cloak—that means about a thousand dollars in our money. It has been estimated that the stock of costumes in a theater would sometimes be worth as much as the theater itself. Robert Greene, in *Groatsworth of Wit,* has an actor brag, "My very share in playing apparel will not be sold for two-hundred pounds." In modern times Mr. Belasco followed the example of the Elizabethans in this respect.

The majority of Elizabethan playhouses were open-air theaters, and performances were given in the afternoon; so it would seem on first thought that lighting effects were out of the question. Yet, on second thought we must realize that, in view of the projecting "hut" and the so-called "heavens," the back of the stage must have been pretty dark, especially in the fall and winter season (London is pretty far north). In fact, it was probably necessary to employ artificial lighting in the rear stage, unless darkness was intended. So lighting effects were by no means out of the question. Lightning could be realistically presented; likewise the "exhalations whizzing in the air" that enabled Brutus to read without a taper. Even the unusual phenomena that disturbed the sky on that momentous night before the assassination of Julius Caesar, terrifying Casca and exhilarating Cassius—even these did not stump the stage-manager. For had not fireworks been recently introduced into England? These made an exhibition of comets and shooting stars an easy matter.

. Sound effects were very popular. Not only was thunder imitated (that was easy), but the songs of birds and the voices of various animals (the barking of dogs, for instance) were reproduced with extraordinary naturalness. The feat was accomplished by means of toys that any boy could buy in London shops. Bells were frequently sounded in plays. There were bells in various parts of the building, and one large bell in the hut: When they were all sounded together (as in *Macbeth* after the discovery of the murder of Duncan), the effect must have been stupendous.

There was machinery to make supernatural beings appear and disappear through trap-doors, and up in the hut there was a mechanism for lowering and hoisting gods and goddesses through the ceiling of the stage. The divinity would sit in a chair which was suspended from a rope. This crude device apparently satisfied the Elizabethan audience; yet some of the effects to which it was treated would tax the resources of the best equipped modern theater. For instance, a hail-storm was rendered with striking verisimilitude by means of small lumps of starch, and a rainstorm was produced with greater realism than would be tolerated by modern actors.

Scenery there was none to speak of. Localities were sufficiently indicated by the conversation and the action. Sometimes the imagination might be helped out by the presence of some property—a tree, or a bank of moss, or a bed, etc. Sometimes a placard would be set up to tell the place, in imitation of the practice in the court masques. Since professional actors were engaged for the court entertainments, it is probable that they carried away some ideas with them. Yet the temptation to imitate the practices of the court would be effectually checked by the expense and the absence of a public demand. Some simple conventions sufficed to give the imagination of the Elizabethan audience all the assistance it wanted. As a play was normally written in blank verse, a rhyme served to announce that the scene had come to an end. An exit at one door, followed by the entrance of a new character or set of characters at another, meant a change of scene. Such devices did not cost anything, and they satisfied the audience.

However unimpressive an Elizabethan performance may appear to us, to the Elizabethan it was a grand spectacle. This we learn from Stephen Gosson, who, in his *Plays Confuted in Five Actions,* has this to say: "So subtile is the devil that under the color of recreation in London and of exercise of learning in the universities, by seeing of plays he maketh us to join with the gentiles in their corruption . . . For the eye, beside the beauty of the houses and the stages, he sendeth in garish apparel, makes vaunting, tumbling, dancing of jigs, galliards, morrises, hobby horses; nothing forgot that might serve to set out the matter with pomp, or ravish the beholder with variety of pleasure. . . . The preparation of stages, apparel, and such like as setteth out our plays in shows of pomp and state, is it that we wonder and gaze at." Gosson had himself written plays for the public theater, so his statement may be accepted as not being the wild utterance of an ignorant enemy of the theater, that is, so far as the total effect is concerned. When he describes the apparel as garish, he does speak as the prejudiced enemy. The Elizabethan producer placed his trust mainly on the costuming. To Orazio Busino, chaplain of the Venetian Embassy, the apparel did not look garish. He tells us that the tragedy he witnessed at the Fortune Theater "diverted me very little, especially as I cannot understand a word of English; though some little amusement may be derived from gazing at the very costly dresses of the actors." Coming from Venice he was a good judge. And we recall Coryat's observation that the playhouses in Venice were "beggarly and bare in comparison of our stately playhouses in England: neither can their actors compare with us for stately apparel, shows, or music." Always the apparel is emphasized.

NOTE. It is only proper to explain that the stage described in the foregoing chapter is a conjectural reconstruction, based on the investigations of scholars during the present century. Though it has met with general acceptance a violently dissenting voice has been raised by Dr. Leslie Hotson, who presents the case for a radically different reconstruction in his book entitled *Shakespeare's Wooden O.* Even if one is not ready to subscribe to his findings they cannot lightly be brushed aside. It must be admitted that the accepted reconstruction does not satisfactorily answer all the questions. Neither does Dr. Hotson's. More research is in order before there can be universal agreement on the subject.

XIII. GOING TO THE THEATER IN SHAKESPEARE'S TIME

The loquacious Parolles, in *All's Well That End's Well,* aiming to express contempt for the military prowess of a certain gentleman, declares: "Faith, sir, has led the drum before the English tragedians." The reference is to a custom practiced by theatrical troupes of holding a procession upon arrival in a town where they were scheduled to perform—as the circus does in our time. In London, where a few companies were permanently established, and plays were of daily occurrence, the announcement of a performance meant less of a holiday, so the parade could be dispensed with. It was sufficient to post bills all over town before nine o'clock on the morning of the performance. John Taylor, the Water Poet, reports this anecdote:

> Master Field, the player, riding up Fleetstreet a great pace, a gentleman called him, and asked him what play was played that day: he (being angry to be stayed upon so frivolous a demand) answered, that he might see what play was to be played upon every post.

The advertisement was supplemented by a drum-beat and three trumpet calls in the afternoon, a little before the play began. The fathers of London City were Puritans, and tolerated the theater only because they could not help themselves, the theater being favored by the royal court. It seems that the drum-beat and the trumpet call got on their nerves, particularly; accordingly, in 1594, they made Shakespeare's company agree not to resort to these loud measures. Nevertheless we know that these loud measures were still resorted to years later. If the actors had not found a way of evading most of the decrees against them there would have been no theater in England.

We are lucky enough to have a copy of one of the playbills of those days—the oldest extant example of a playbill of an English play. It derives added interest from the fact that it comes from Germany and is printed in the German language; for it is a forcible reminder of the fact that the English companies were famous outside of England, and made frequent tours of the continent. The poster we have comes from Nuremberg, dated April 21, 1628, and, translated, reads:

> Be it known to all that there has arrived here a brand new company

of comedians, such as have never yet been seen in this country, with a very merry clown; which company will give daily performances of fine Comedies, Tragedies, Pastorals, and Histories; also enjoyable and merry Interludes; and today, Wednesday, the 21st of April, they will present a very merry Comedy, entitled LOVE'S SWEETNESS TRANSFORMED TO DEATH'S BITTERNESS. After the Comedy there will be presented a beautiful Ballet and a funny farce. Lovers of such plays will please be in their places at two o'clock in the afternoon at the Boxing Hall, · as the performance will begin promptly at the time specified.

The title of the play would aptly fit Shakespeare's *Romeo and Juliet.* It may seem odd that a play with such a theme should be called a "merry Comedy"; yet it is clear that strolling players were guilty of such absurdities, and that Peter Quince had good professional authority for calling *Pyramus and Thisbe* a "Lamentable Comedy." It also seems clear that Polonius was quoting a playbill when he sang the praises of the troupe that came to entertain Hamlet.

Plays were normally given in the afternoon. This was the traditional custom, therefore it seemed the only rational practice. Certainly circumstances were not calculated to develop the idea of evening performances. The danger of walking through London's unlighted streets at night would alone have sufficed to discourage the idea. As it was, the afternoon seemed the only fitting and proper time for plays. A writer of that day says of the actor: "He entertains us in the best leisure of our life—that is, between meals; the most unfit time for study or bodily exercise." Is the modern custom, which sends people to bed after midnight, a more rational one?

Performances were usually scheduled to begin at two o'clock. As seats were not reserved the audience would begin to arrive long ahead of time to secure the best places, and it must frequently have happened that the performance did not begin promptly—perhaps because the players were not ready, perhaps the house was not full enough. Ben Jonson humorously makes a spectator say, "I wish they would begin once; this protraction is able to sour the best-settled patience in the theater!" To keep their patience from "souring" the spectators might play cards, or regale themselves on some of the numerous things peddled in the playhouse, such as apples, nuts, tobacco, ale. In Fletcher's

Woman Hater we are told that the nervous author "stands peeping between the curtains so fearfully that a bottle of ale cannot be opened but he thinks somebody hisses." Even books were on sale, if one had a mind for reading. If it happened to be one of the better theaters the delay would probably be filled in by the musicians, for the English people had a passion for music. The musical contingent was always a large proportion of the whole company. In an English troupe totaling fifteen, that played in Strassburg in 1605, seven were musicians. Each member of the orchestra was probably ready to play on more than one instrument. In an account of an English troupe that visited Münster in 1599, we read that "they had with them many different instruments, such as lutes, zithers, viols, and the like."

The music was undoubtedly of the best quality. The Duke of Stettin-Pomerania found that the audience gathered in the Blackfriars Theater long before the performance was scheduled to begin, in order to enjoy the musical program, for the merit of which he has the highest praise. The good-natured highwayman, Gamaliel Ratsey, addressing the leader of a troupe of strolling players that he was planning to hold up, demanded: "I pray you, let me have your music, for I have often gone to plays more for music sake than for action." A writer in 1644 (after the closing of the theaters by the Puritans) speaks reminiscently of "the very music between each act" being worth more than the puppet plays which were still tolerated. He goes on to tell us that the musicians at Blackfriars (Shakespeare's theater) were "esteemed the best of common musicians in London."

When the playgoer arrived at the theater, he paid a general admission fee of one penny—two pence if it was a new play—that entitled him to standing room in the pit, or yard, as they called it. If he did not wish to sort with the "groundlings" he would walk over to the stairway that led to the balconies and pay the additional fee required for the seat he desired. If he was a dandy, who had just bought a new cloak, or had just dyed his whiskers the latest shade, or who, for any reason whatever, wished to be seen rather than to see, he would come in by the stage entrance and sit on the stage, paying sixpence for the privilege.

Prices of admission varied. In the open-air theaters the lowest price seems to have been one penny (top wages for skilled journeyman were 6s. a week) and the highest one shilling. In the indoor theaters, which were decidedly more select, and where there was no standing room the range appears to have been from threepence to five shillings.

Once the performance got started it would, in the normal course of events, proceed to the end as it does today. Now and then, however, the performance was interrupted by the capture of a pickpocket, who would be unceremoniously hustled up on the stage, tied to one of the pillars supporting the overhanging superstructure, and left there till the end of the performance, to be jeered at in convenient intervals.

Sometimes, toward the end of the performance, when the money "gatherers" had left their posts, stragglers would sneak in to enjoy the little vaudeville diversion that was pretty sure to follow the play. This diversion would consist of song, dance, and farcial dialogue, and was known as a "jig."

The afternoon would be brought to a close by one of the actors coming forward and announcing the play for the next day; for normally the same play was not given two days in succession. A new play was considered a success if it could attract an audience once a week for a season. After the accession of James, however, when all the companies came under the direct patronage of the royal family, the announcement would be preceded by all the actors coming out on the stage and kneeling in prayer for their patron.

What a passion the theater was with the Londoner may be gathered from preacher John Stockwood's pathetic complaint quoted on page 87 in a sermon he preached in 1578. And this passion must have augmented with time, for a quarter of a century later the author of *Virtue's Commonwealth* informs us that "many poor, pinched, needy creatures that live on alms and have scarce neither cloth for their back nor food for their belly, yet will make hard shift but they will see a play, let wife and children beg and languish in penury."

XIV.   SHAKESPEARE'S AUDIENCE

We are fortunate in having numerous contemporary descriptions which give us a graphic picture of the Elizabethan audience. In Middleton and Rowley's *Roaring Girl* we get a view of the auditorium of the Fortune Theater from the stage:

> . . . men and women, mixed together;
> Fair ones with foul, like sunshine in wet weather.
> Within one square a thousand heads are laid,
> So close that all of heads the room seems made. . .
> And here and there, whilst with obsequious ears
> Throng'd heaps do listen, a cutpurse thrusts and leers
> With hawk's eyes for his prey. . . Then, sir, below,
> The very floor, as 'twere, waves to and fro,
> And like a floating island, seems to move
> Upon a sea bound in with shores above.

This is a very general description. Effective details are supplied by the chaplain of the Venetian embassy, who visited the Fortune in 1617: "The best treat was to see such a crowd of nobility so very well arrayed that they looked like so many princes, listening as silently and soberly as possible. These theaters are frequented by a number of respectable ladies, who come freely and seat themselves among the men without the slightest hesitation."

The chaplain of course sat in one of the expensive parts of the house. A less attractive picture is presented by the "groundlings"; that is, the crowds that swarmed the part of the theater now called the orchestra, but was then, more appropriately, called the pit. Since there were no seats in this part of the house there was less practical restriction to crowding, so that on occasion it must have been uncomfortably jammed. We are told that in a good season the playhouses "smoked every afternoon with stinkards that were so glued together in crowds with the steams of strong breath, that when they came forth, their faces looked as if they had been parboiled." Dekker, addressing the actors, says: "Ye shall be glad to play three hours for twopence to the basest stinkards in London, whose breath is stronger than garlic, and able to poison all the twelve-penny rooms."

The indoor theaters were more exclusive, the high prices

serving to keep the "tag-rag people" away. The contrast is
brought out by Marston, speaking of the playhouse in which the
Paul's Boys acted, in *Jack Drum's Entertainment:*

> In faith, I like the audience that frequenteth there
> With much applause. A man shall not be chok'd
> With the stench of garlic, nor be pasted
> To the barmy jacket of a beer-brewer.

This reminds one of Casca's account in *Julius Caesar:* "The
rabblement hooted, and clapp'd their hands, and threw up their
sweaty nightcaps, and utter'd such a deal of stinking breath that
it had almost chok'd Caesar; for he swounded at it: and for my
part, I durst not laugh, for fear of opening my lips and receiving
the bad air." Undoubtedly Shakespeare used his own audience
as a model for the Roman mob. In fact, in the continuation of
his report Casca declares: "If the tag-rag people did not clap him
and hiss him according as he pleased and displeased them, as
they use to do the players in the theater, I am no true man." We
may suspect that the audiences at the indoor theaters were not
quite so ideally constituted as Marston would have us believe. In
a petition by the indoor theater actors, disemployed by the
closing of all theaters in 1642, they promise, if allowed to
reopen, "never to admit into our six-penny rooms those
unwholesome, enticing harlots, that sit there merely to be taken
up by prentices or lawyers' clerks, nor any female of what
degree soever except they come lawfully with their husbands or
near allies." Apparently, also, the stench of perspiration was
there replaced by the obnoxious odor of cheap tobacco, for
they promise that "the abuses in tobacco shall be reformed,
none vended, nor so much as in three-penny galleries, unless of
the pure Spanish leaf."

The most picturesque part of the audience was the group of
gallants that occupied stools on the stage. They were there to
show off—either their dress, or their wit, or both. Their wit
would be exercised in criticizing the play and the actors. Writers
of the day lose no opportunity to poke ridicule at their
ostentation. Even the editors of the First Folio refer to them as
"magistrates of wit, who sit on the stage to arraign plays daily;"
and Dekker humorously tells "How a gallant should behave

himself in a playhouse." He should wait until the very last minute before the play begins, and then suddenly creep from behind the curtains with a three-footed stool in one hand, and the extra fee of sixpence in the other, paying no attention to "the mews and hisses of the opposed rascality." At inappropriate moments in the course of the play he should let the house ring with laughter, and finally, he should rise in the middle of the performance "with a screwed and discontented face" and leave with a number of friends. The actors will then be thankful to him for "allowing them elbow room." The fact is, however, that neither actors nor authors were thankful when this happened, as we learn from Chapman's Prologue to *All Fools.* A play that was thus visibly disapproved by the self-constituted jury of dandies on the stage, was very apt to be hopelessly damned in the eyes of the rest of the audience.

Between the acts there was naturally plenty of noise. In *Henry the Eighth,* the rowdy multitude that is trying to force its way into the palace to witness the christening of the infant Elizabeth is referred to as "the youths that thunder at a playhouse and fight for bitten apples, that no audience . . . are able to endure." The spectators would lay in a supply of meats and drinks and tobacco that were loudly hawked through the house; and we have reason to fear that the consumption of these articles was not limited to the intermissions. The smoking was incessant, and we are told that sometimes the hiss caused by the opening of a bottle was mistaken by the actor for a hiss of disapproval. On one occasion, indeed, a spectator's foresight possibly saved his life. When the Globe Theater burned down, in 1613, a man's clothes took fire, and he had presence of mind to extinguish the flame with a bottle of ale that he had provided himself with. On the whole, however, the silent and sober attention which the Venetian chaplain observed was probably characteristic of the Elizabethan audience generally. On occasion, of course, it could behave in anything but refined fashion. The Prologue to Taylor's *The Hog Hath Lost His Pearl* fears that:

> We may be pelted off, for aught we know,
> With apples, eggs, or stones, from those below.

Such conduct was not confined to "those below." The head of Tarleton, the famous comedian of Shakespeare's early days in London, once stopped the course of an apple that came sailing from one of the galleries. Usually, however, disapproval was expressed by mewing and hissing.

Since the traits of the population exert a dominant influence on what an author writes, let us hear what the German traveler, Paul Hentzner, observed on his trip to England in 1598. He tells us that the English were serious like the Germans: lovers of show, good dancers and musicians, politer in eating than the French, taking less bread, more meat, and much sugar in their drink, quick of body and wit, good sailors and better pirates. "They are powerful in the field, successful against their enemies, impatient of anything like slavery, and vastly fond of great noises that fill the ear, such as the firing of cannon, drums, and the ringing of bells; so that it is common for a number of them, that have got a glass in their heads, to go up into some belfry and ring the bells for hours together, for the sake of exercise."

He might have added that they took delight in scenes of violence and cruelty; but in this respect they did not differ from other Europeans of those times.

These are the people for whom Shakespeare wrote. If we keep them in mind we shall understand his plays better.

XV.   WILLIAM SHAKESPEARE

William Shakespeare was baptized at Stratford-on-Avon April 26, 1564. The favorite conjecture is that he was born April 23, simply because he died on April 23. The occasion calls for humble thanksgiving, for the plague was carrying away the babies of Stratford at the time, but spared the infant that was to be the greatest playwright of all time. On his father's side he was descended from the Norman invaders; on his mother's side directly from King Alfred. Besides, a few generations back a Celtic strain had entered the family bloodstream on his mother's side. Surely then, if there is anything in heredity, the possibility of Shakespeare's developing a universal outlook on life was not diminished by his descent.

His father, John Shakespeare, was a glover by trade, and like other glovers at the time, engaged in the wool business generally. Precisely when he came to Stratford is not known, but he was there in 1552, for there is a record in that year of his being fined for not clearing away the garbage from before his door. In 1557 he married Mary Arden, daughter of a wealthy farmer in Snittersfield, four miles away. He must have known Mary from childhood, as his father had been her father's tenant. The Ardens belonged to the gentry, and when she married a man who was not a "gentleman," in the English sense of the word, she too, according to the law, forfeited her coat-of-arms, and ceased to be a "gentlewoman." But the man she married was evidently an intelligent and prosperous citizen, highly respected in the community. For many years he was alderman, and for ten years even high bailiff (or mayor) of the town.

The first two children were girls, who died in infancy. The third was William. Later three sons and two daughters were born. There was a grammar school in Stratford, which William began to attend when he was seven, as was customary. The course was a seven-year course, but they must have covered much more ground than we do in seven years; for the school sessions were from seven in the morning to five in the afternoon, with a two-hour recess from eleven to one. In some schools the sessions were from six to six, and that may have been the case in Stratford. Latin was the most important subject in the curriculum, and when Shakespeare finished school he probably knew as much Latin as a Harvard graduate does today. That would not mean much to such a scholar as Ben Jonson, who taunted Shakespeare with having "small Latin and less Greek." However, Jonson's taunt simply proves that Greek was among Shakespeare's accomplishments.

The method of discipline was Ichabod Crane's method: they took care not to spoil the child. In his attitude toward school William was probably a normal boy, and if we are to judge by his references to school and schoolmasters in his plays, he did not suffer heaviness of heart when the day came that he had to turn his back on school and, as was the usual practice, enter his father's shop as an apprentice.

Those misguided people who doubt Shakespeare's authorship of the plays attributed to him make much of the fact that his formal education terminated with his graduation from Grammar School, while the plays reveal a wide range of knowledge and understanding. Setting aside the foolish implication that knowledge can be acquired only within academic walls, we may rest assured that the mental discipline to which Shakespeare was subjected in his seven years of schooling was sufficient to enable even an ordinary man to pursue his studies on his own. One is tempted to assume that Shakespeare had himself in mind when he wrote about Prince Hal's surprisingly extensive learning. In *King Henry the Fifth* the Archbishop of Canterbury and the Bishop of Ely are discussing the newly crowned young prince:

> *Cant.* Never was such a sudden scholar made. . .
> Hear him but reason in divinity,
> And, all-admiring, with an inward wish
> You would desire the king were made a prelate:
> Hear him debate of commonwealth affairs,
> You would say it hath been all in all his study:
> List his discourse of war, and you shall hear
> A fearful battle render'd you in music:
> Turn him to any cause of policy,
> The Gordian knot of it he will unloose,
> Familiar as his garter; that, when he speaks,
> The air, a charter'd libertine, is still,
> And the mute wonder lurketh in men's ears,
> To steal his sweet and honey'd sentences. . . .
> Which is a wonder how his grace should glean it,

> Since his addiction was to courses vain. . . .
> And never noted in him any study,
> Any retirement, any sequestration,
> From open haunts and popularity.

The Bishop of Ely suggests that appearances must have been deceiving, that the prince must have "obscur'd his contemplation under a veil of wildness." The archbishop acquiesces in this judgment: "It must be so;" he says, "for miracles are past." Shakespeare's diversified, yet substantial, information, then, was the result of no miracle. He repeatedly emphasizes the importance of knowledge. "Folly and ignorance," he declares, are "the common curse of mankind;" and again, "Ignorance is the curse of God, knowledge the wing wherewith we fly to heaven." If that is what knowledge meant to him he must have pursued it passionately.

About this time Stratford began to lose its position as the center of the English wool trade, so John Shakespeare's fortunes started to decline. One after another, through sale or mortgage, he lost the lands his wife had inherited. In these steadily darkening circumstances William's sensitive soul must have craved sunshine, and frequent must have been his rambles to a pretty cottage in Shottery, about a mile away, where a girl's smile awaited him.

At the age of eighteen Shakespeare married the girl, Anne Hathaway by name, and brought her to his father's house. The wedding had to be hastened, for in six months a child was due. She was eight years older than he, and he was only a boy. We can only speculate as to the happiness or unhappiness of their married life. Whatever evidence there is seems to point to uncongeniality. Two passages in his plays warn of the unhappy consequences of premarital intimacy and marrying a woman older than yourself. In *The Tempest* Prospero addresses his prospective son-in-law:

> Then, as my gift, and thine own acquisition
> Worthily purchas'd, take my daughter. But
> If thou dost break her virgin-knot before
> All sanctimonious ceremonies may
> With full and holy rite be minister'd,

> No sweet aspersion shall the heavens let fall
> To make this contract grow; but barren hate,
> Sour-eyed disdain and discord shall bestrew
> The union of your bed with weeds so loathly
> That you shall hate it both.

And in *Twelfth Night,* when Viola, disguised as a boy, admits to the young Duke that she is in love with someone about his age (she *is* in love with the Duke himself) the Duke advises "him":

> Too old, by heaven. Let still the woman take
> An elder than herself; so wears she to him,
> So sways she level in her husband's heart. . . .
> Then let thy love be younger than thyself,
> Or thy affection cannot hold the bent.

Both of these speeches are out of place. Prospero's admonition sounds uncalled-for in relation to the two young people involved, and the Duke's words in *Twelfth Night* are utterly out of keeping with the character Shakespeare has given him. We cannot escape the conclusion that Shakespeare is here indulging in bitter reflections upon his own experience. It is worth noting that the impression we get from the play is that Viola is of the age at which Shakespeare got married, and that the difference in years between her and the Duke is no greater than that between Shakespeare and his wife. Yet the Duke exclaims,"Too old, by heaven."

The number of startling parallels to Shakespeare's own experience is too large and too pointed to be brushed aside as accidental. In *King Lear* the Fool asserts that "He's mad that trusts in the tameness of a wolf, a horse's health, a boy's love"; and in the same play Kent declares that he is "not so young to love a woman for singing." There is no inherent necessity in the play for these observations. When the ardent lover Paris pleads with Juliet's father: "Younger than she are happy mothers made," the latter's response is: "And too soon marr'd are those so early made." In *Henry the Sixth,* Gloucester avers that "Hasty marriage seldom proveth well." The most pointed statement of all appears in *Troilus and Cressida.* There Shakespeare, through Troilus, speaks directly to us in the first person:

> I take today a wife, and my election
> Is led on in the conduct of my will.
> My will enkindled by mine eyes and ears,
> Two traded pilots 'twixt the dangerous shores
> Of will and judgment: how may I avoid,
> Although my will distaste what it elected,
> The wife I chose? There can be no evasion
> To blench from this and to stand firm by honor.

Could anything be more pat? I am afraid we cannot do otherwise than accept the autobiographical significance of these passages. Besides, we cannot ignore the simple fact that he left his wife in Stratford and lived many years in London alone. Incidentally, it is noteworthy that both Kent and Troilus speak of the alluring power of a woman's singing. May we not surmise that Anne Hathaway had a beautiful voice, and that the lad William had his "will enkindled" by her singing? We know that Shakespeare loved music.

Surely, the generous visits of the stork, that brought first a girl and then a girl plus a boy as twins, to the impoverished and overcrowded home, could not be hailed as an unmixed blessing. Shakespeare was still an apprentice, and the increase in the family was not accompanied by a corresponding increase in the family revenue.

At twenty-one his period of apprenticeship was over, and he was free to turn to anything he pleased. There is fair ground for believing that he sought to provide for his wife and three children by teaching school in the neighborhood of Stratford. Again, if we are to judge by his portraits of schoolmasters, he did not find the occupation a congenial one. There was only one thing that called him, heart and soul—the theater. When his father was mayor of Stratford the best London companies were welcomed there, so he had opportunities to see them play. In May, 1587, when Leicester's Men stopped at the town in their tour of the provinces, he probably burned his bridges behind him and joined them.

What work was assigned to him at the beginning is not known. He was probably apprenticed to the prompter to assist him in his manifold duties. The law required a seven-year period of apprenticeship, irrespective of age. It did not take him long, however, to prove his ability both as actor and as playwright. The first definite reference to him in London dates from 1592, in the form of an envious attack on him by Robert Greene, who accused him of stealing from his works. He called him an "upstart crow beautified with our feathers." Thanks to this attack we are in possession of the first, indeed the fullest, pen portrait of Shakespeare that has come down to us from a contemporary. *A Groatsworth of Wit,* in which the attack appeared, was written while Greene was sick in bed, in fact on his death bed. Greene at best had a wretched handwriting, so his friend Henry Chettle arranged for its publication, and prepared a legible copy for the printer. This led to his being accused of being its author. In his published disclaimer Chettle declared: "I am sorry as if the original fault had been my fault, because myself have seen his demeanor no less civil than he excellent in the quality he professes. Besides, divers of worship have reported his uprightness of dealing, which argues his honesty, and his facetious grace in writing that approves his art."

From personal knowledge, then, Chettle spoke of Shakespeare's gentlemanly behavior and his skill as an actor (for "quality" means profession). Furthermore, he tells us that in the opinion of those whose word counted, Shakespeare was upright in his dealings with men, and able as a writer.

His seven years of formal apprenticeship must have been prosperous ones, for in 1594, on the expiration of his term, he was in a position to buy a full share in his company, then known as Lord Strange's Company, thus opening up a lucrative source of income.

From his sonnets we know that Shakespeare keenly felt the stigma attaching to his occupation as an actor. He made up his mind to make use of his increasing funds by purchasing back the place among the gentry that his mother had lost when she married his father. In 1596, in his father's name, he applied to the Herald's Office for a coat-of-arms. By making the application in his father's name, and not his own, he accomplished two things: first, he simplified the red-tape connected with the procedure, for John Shakespeare's election, in 1571, to the office of chief alderman, made him eligible for a coat-of-arms; second, by elevating his father to the gentry he enabled his mother to recover the coat-of-arms she forfeited when she married. His application was granted, and three years later he applied for the privilege of quartering his arms with those of the Ardens. His ambition, which was never to be realized, was to establish an English "family." An English family is founded on land and is maintained through generations of sons. The first check to his ambition came in the very year when he acquired his first coat-of-arms. His only son, Hamnet, then in his twelfth year, died. This terrible blow did not, however, kill his hope. In the following year he purchased the finest house in Stratford, and brought suit (without success) to recover his mother's estate forfeited through mortgage, and to the end of his days he kept investing his money in land. Even if no more sons came to him there was still the possibility that his two daughters would give him grandsons. But fate was not kind to him. His elder daughter Susanna, gave birth to a girl, Elizabeth, whose first and second marriage both proved childless. The story of his younger daughter, Judith, is even more sad. She gave birth to a son, whom she called Shakespeare, to assure the perpetuation of the name; but he died in infancy. She then had two more sons, who grew to young manhood, and then were swept away together by the plague. Thus, one dream of Shakespeare, who gave reality to many dreams, was never materialized. His line terminated with the death of his grand-daughter, Elizabeth, who passed away in 1670, at the age of sixty-two.

In other respects, however, fortune smiled on him. In 1598, Francis Meres speaks of him as the greatest writer in the country, a position that must already have been recognized as his for some time. About the same time, the Cambridge students, in the University play, *Return from Parnassus,* refer to him as "sweet Mr. Shakespeare."

In 1598, likewise, he joined a syndicate to build a new playhouse, the Globe, on the Bankside, to take the place of The Theater, in Shoreditch. By the arrangement he became one-tenth owner. Ten years later he similarly became part owner of the Blackfriars Theater.

In 1601 Shakespeare took up his lodging on Silver Street, with a wig-maker named Mountjoy. While living there he had the opportunity to play a role that he evidently loved—that of match-maker. He was instrumental in bringing about the marriage of Mountjoy's daughter to his apprentice.

In the same year an event occurred that probably was the severest shock of his life. His father died. The first play written after this event was *Hamlet;* and we are justified in finding an autobiographical element in the relation between Hamlet and his father. Hamlet's grief was Shakespeare's grief; Hamlet's words about his father: "take him for all in all, I shall not look upon his like again," were a tribute to his own father, whose golden qualities made him the most respected citizen in Stratford.

In the remaining years of his life there was surely plenty of sunshine, but also plenty of shadow. In 1606, William Davenant, who was destined to play an important part in re-establishing the drama after the Restoration, was named after him. In the following year his elder daughter, Susanna, made an excellent match in her marriage to Dr. John Hall. But the same year also brought the death of his youngest brother, Edmund, who had been acting with him in London. A year later, a daughter was born to the Hall's—the only grandchild Shakespeare lived to see. But the Reaper did not follow far behind the stork, and carried away his mother.

His achievement as a dramatist continued to rise to new heights, but his production slowed up, and ceased finally in 1611, with *The Tempest.* He was then only forty-seven years old, and his work showed no diminishing of power. But he probably felt that the current of the age was turning against him, as it had been for some years, now that the forces of the Renaissance were rapidly spending themselves. Like Prospero, in his last play, he concluded that there was no longer any urgent call for the exercise of his magical powers, and that it was as well to break his magic wand and bury his magic books. Prospero's serenity, too, we may take as representing Shakespeare's state of mind. There was no bitterness accompanying his early retirement. His soul was too lofty to admit of any.

Notwithstanding the death of his two remaining brothers, Gilbert and Richard, in 1612 and 1613 respectively, we may assume that the remaining years of Shakespeare's life were years of peace. His financial circumstances were more than comfortable, for he had used his money wisely. He probably spent most of his time with his wife and children in Stratford, but he did not completely separate himself from affairs in London. In the winter of 1612-13 he helped Fletcher (whose collaborator, Beaumont, had retired) write *Henry VIII,* and in the same year the Earl of Rutland engaged him to devise a symbolic emblem with an appropriate motto for his shield.

He died April 23, 1616; but three months before he closed his eyes he at last had the joy of seeing his younger daughter, Judith, now thirty-two, married.

As mentioned above, Shakespeare's line ended with the death of his grand-daughter in 1670. But his father's line did not terminate then. The descendents of his sister Joan are now scattered throughout the world, including America.

It may be worth while mentioning that the dramatic instinct in the family did not die with Shakespeare. Both his nephew, William Hart, and his grand-nephew, Charles Hart, eventually joined the company to which he had belonged. After the reopening of the theaters at the Restoration, Charles Hart became one of the most famous actors in England.

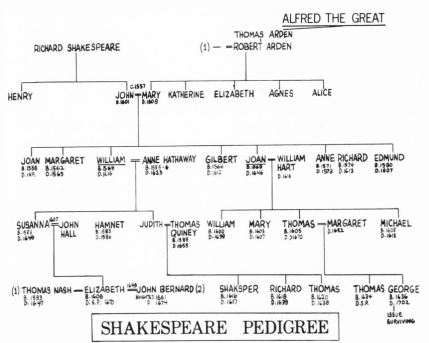

SHAKESPEARE PEDIGREE

XVI. SHAKESPEARE'S DEVELOPMENT AS A PLAYWRIGHT

The following chronology of Shakespeare's plays is based on the findings of Professor Thomas Whitfield Baldwin. When a play is listed twice, the later date marks a revision.

1588, winter, Love's Labor's Lost
1589, summer, Love's Labor's Won (earlier version of All's Well)
1589, winter, Comedy of Errors
1590, summer, Two Gentlemen of Verona
1590, winter, Henry V
1591, summer, Romeo and Juliet
1591, winter, 1 Henry VI
1591, winter, 2 Henry VI
1591, winter, 3 Henry VI
1592, summer, Titus Andronicus

The next four plays were prepared while Shakespeare's company was touring the provinces on account of the plague in London.

1592, winter, Jealous Comedy (earlier version of Merry Wives)
1593, summer, Hamlet
1593, winter, Richard III
1594, summer, Midsummer Night's Dream
1594, winter, Taming of the Shrew
1595, summer, King John
1595, winter, Richard II
1596, summer, 1 Henry IV
1596, winter, 2 Henry IV
1597, summer, Merchant of Venice
1597, winter, Love's Labor's Lost
1598, summer, Romeo and Juliet
1598, winter, Much Ado about Nothing
1599, summer, Henry V
1599, winter, Julius Caesar
1600, summer, As You Like It
1600, winter, Twelfth Night
1601, summer, Troilus and Cressida

1601-1603, *Theaters closed on account of plague.*
1603, summer, Hamlet
1603, winter, Merry Wives of Windsor
1604, summer, Othello
1604, winter, Measure for Measure
1605, summer, Timon of Athens
1605, winter, King Lear
1606, summer, Macbeth
1606, winter, Antony and Cleopatra
1607, summer, All's Well That Ends Well
1607, summer, Pericles (with Wilkens and Fletcher)
1608, summer, Coriolanus
1610, winter, Cymbeline
1611, summer, Winter's Tale
1611, winter, Tempest
1612, winter, Henry VIII (with Fletcher)

A careful scrutiny of the order of Shakespeare's plays reveals the fact that, in a general way, his dramatic activity may be divided into five periods. When Shakespeare arrived in London, Lyly had been writing for some years for companies of children that catered to select audiences at court and in indoor theaters. The first four plays of Shakespeare show Lyly's influence. The prompt way in which Shakespeare fell under that influence justifies the assumption that Lyly had established a vogue which the public theaters were eager to follow; for a playwright could not write merely to please himself, but to please the company that would buy his play. While Shakespeare was writing these four plays–light comedies all of them–two men, Thomas Kyd and Christopher Marlowe, were taking the theatrical world by storm; the former with his *Spanish Tragedy,* a violent tragedy of blood and revenge; the latter with his *Tamburlaine* and *Doctor Faustus,* presenting heaven-and-earth defying epic heroes. But Shakespeare could not then come under their influence, for the simple reason that their plays were acted while he was busy in his own theater. But Lyly's plays it was possible for him to see performed; for the Paul's Boys, who acted them, did not begin their performances before four o'clock, after religious services were over. Indeed, Lyly's earliest plays were in print, and it is hard to believe that Shakespeare had not read them–the best plays by far that had yet been written in the English language. It is not unlikely that the reading of these plays while he was engaged in uncongenial work to support his family, opened his eyes to his own possibilities and caused London to beckon to him.

In 1590, however, a temporary association between his company and the Admiral's Men brought the plays of Kyd and Marlowe to his own theater, as well as those of Robert Greene, who began as an imitator of Marlowe. For the next three years Shakespeare's company kept him busy revising and imitating the work of these three and their disciples. It was his success in this work that provoked Greene's envious attack on him. Most of the plays of this period belong to the type known as the Chronicle Play, or History–the most popular type at the time, most popular, probably, because of the elation following the defeat of Spain. Nash, writing in 1592, says that the substance of the plays then in vogue was, "for the most part, borrowed out of our English chronicles, wherein our forefathers' valiant acts are revived." This second period in Shakespeare's dramatic career terminates in 1593, with *Richard III.*

The third period ends with *Twelfth Night,* in 1600. It is essentially one of romantic comedy. It marks a resumption of work begun with *The Two Gentlemen of Verona.*

The fourth period comes to a close in 1608, with *Coriolanus.* This is the period of the great tragedies. Shakespeare's dramatic activity during this period runs counter to, rather than parallel with, the current of dramatic activity of the time. The powerful Renaissance spirit had spent its force with the closing years of the sixteenth century. The circumstances which had made all England, from court to peasantry, one body and soul, were no longer operative. The nation began to settle down to conventional conformity. The theater, as was inevitable, reflected the spirit of the new age. Shakespeare, however, remained self-dependent. His genius propelled itself on the impetus which it had been accumulating from the day he began to write. While the work of his contemporaries was marked by decadence, his rose to new heights–the loftiest in the history of the drama.

The fifth, and last, period is the period of tragi-comic romances. It begins in 1610, Shakespeare having taken a two-year vacation in Stratford, probably feeling that he was through. The type of work done in the fifth period was determined by the fact that in 1608 Shakespeare's company took possession of the Blackfriars Theater, which the Children of the Queen's Revels (under various names) had occupied since 1600. It now behooved the new occupants to supply the patrons of this theater with the kind of play that they had been accustomed to witness, which meant a play which, while exciting, was not too serious, and which had a goodly share of music, dancing, and show; in other words, the type of play whose traditional development traced back to the time when the children's troupes played exclusively for the court. To assure a supply of this kind of play, the company retained the services of Beaumont and Fletcher, who had already written for the Blackfriars audience. When Shakespeare was persuaded to come back in 1610, he followed in their footsteps. That the new type did not faze him is proved by the fact that his last uncollaborated play, *The Tempest,* is not merely the greatest play of its kind; it is one of the greatest of Shakespeare's works.

The last play on the list is only partly Shakespeare's. It rightly belongs to Fletcher. He had been accustomed to write in collaboration with Beaumont. Now that Beaumont had retired from the theater, Fletcher must have felt insecure; so Shakespeare agreed to help him out.

The Elizabethan playwrights, like the playwrights of today, thought of their product as something to be performed in a theater before a contemporary audience. They did not think of readers, nor did they think of posterity. It is not surprising, then, that Shakespeare did not see to it that his plays were published. They did not belong to him anyhow. They were the property of the company, to whom he had sold them. If a play was published, it was the company that had disposed of it to the printer. John Marston voiced the attitude of his time when he declared: "One thing afflicts me, to think that scenes invented merely to be spoken should be published to be read"; and, "Remember, the life of these things consists in action." Ben Jonson, however, entered a dissenting voice. To him drama was literature. It was Aeschylus, Sophocles, Euripides, Aristophanes; and he had the vision to link Shakespeare's name with theirs, and declare that "He was not of an age but for all time." Needless to say, Jonson thought the same of himself, so he carefully edited an edition of his dramas, which he significantly called "works," not "plays." But Shakespeare did not possess the scholar's attitude that was Jonson's, and he certainly lacked the latter's self-consciousness. He felt that if posterity remembered him at all, it would be through his non-dramatic work, like the sonnets, which *were* literature, in one of which he avers:

> . . . Death to me subscribes,
> Since, spite of him, I'll live in this poor rhyme.

Indeed, any claim which the plays might file to being literature is explicitly denied in Shakespeare's dedication of his poem, *Venus and Adonis,* to the Earl of Southampton, printed in 1593. He calls it "the first heir of my invention," though he had written a number of plays before.

Only half of Shakespeare's plays were printed during his lifetime. Had it not been for the loving care of two of his fellow actors, John Heminge and Henry Condell, who published his complete works in the First Folio of 1623, seven years after his death, the world would never have been enriched with the other half. What a debt of eternal gratitude humanity owes these two men!

[121]

LIST OF BOOKS

Adams, J. C. The Globe Playhouse. Harvard U. Press
Adams, J. Q. A Life of William Shakespeare. Houghton Mifflin
—— Shakespearean Playhouses. Houghton Mifflin
Baldwin, T. W. The Organization and Personnel of the Shakespearean Company. Princeton U. Press
Boas, F. S. University Drama in the Tudor Age. Clarendon Press
—— Five Pre-Shakespearean Comedies. Oxford U. Press
Brooke, C. F. T. Tudor Drama. Houghton Mifflin
Chambers, E. K. The Mediaeval Stage. Clarendon Press
—— The Elizabethan Stage. Clarendon Press
—— William Shakespeare. Oxford
Craig, Hardin. English Religious Drama. Clarendon Press
Everyman's Library. Everyman, with Other Interludes
—— The Minor Elizabethan Drama
Harbage, Alfred. Shakespeare's Audience. Columbia U. Press
Hotson, L. Shakespeare's Wooden O. Rupert Hart-Davis
Manly, J. M. Specimens of the Pre-Shakespearean Drama. Ginn
Murray, J. T. English Dramatic Companies. Constable
Schelling, F. E. Elizabethan Drama. Houghton Mifflin
Shakespeare's England. An Account of the Life and Manners of His Age. Clarendon Press
Wallace, C. W. The Evolution of the English Drama up to Shakespeare. Nebraska U. Press

Index